A Guy's Guide to the Good Life

ROBERT P. LOCKWOOD

*A GUY'S
GUIDE
TO THE
GOOD LIFE*

VIRTUES FOR MEN

SERVANT
BOOKS

PUBLISHED BY ST. ANTHONY MESSENGER PRESS
CINCINNATI, OHIO

Excerpts from *Dante Alighieri's Divine Comedy* (Vol. 1–2, ©1997), (Vol. 3–4, ©2000), (Vol. 5–6, ©2005), translated by Mark Musa, reprinted with permission of Indiana University Press.

Unless otherwise noted, Scripture passages have been taken from the *Revised Standard Version*, Catholic edition. Copyright 1946, 1952, 1971 by the Division of Christian Education of the National Council of Churches of Christ in the USA. Used by permission. All rights reserved.

Excerpts from the English translation of the *Catechism of the Catholic Church* for the United States of America, copyright ©1994 Libreria Editrice Vaticana—United States Catholic Conference, Inc. Used with permission. Excerpts from the English translation of the *Catechism of the Catholic Church: Modifications From the* Editio Typica, copyright ©1994 Libreria Editrice Vaticana—United States Catholic Conference, Inc.

Cover and book design by Mark Sullivan

LIBRARY OF CONGRESS CATALOGING-IN-PUBLICATION DATA
Lockwood, Robert P.
A guy's guide to the good life : the virtues for men / Robert P. Lockwood.
p. cm.
Includes bibliographical references.
ISBN 978-0-86716-867-9 (pbk. : alk. paper) 1. Virtues. 2. Men—Conduct of life.
I. Title.
BV4630.L63 2009
241'.042—dc22
2009002531

ISBN 978-0-86716-867-9

Published by Servant Books, an imprint of
St. Anthony Messenger Press.
28 W. Liberty St.
Cincinnati, OH 45202
www.ServantBooks.org

Printed in the United States of America.
Printed on acid-free paper.

11 12 13 5 4 3 2

This one is for my twins:
Ryan and Theresa
Liam and Ethan

CONTENTS

A NOTE OF THANKS

.

.

.

.

.

.

.

Authors pretend that they are the creators of books, but they know they are just cogs in the wheel. Or at least I know that.

This book came to be because the national Catholic newspaper *Our Sunday Visitor* has given me space for many years to ramble on and on. I have so many friends at *Our Sunday Visitor*—old and new—that it would be impossible to list them individually. So I thank them all.

Mike Aquilina—prolific Catholic author and one who has the gift for living the virtues every day—nudged me into this one. And then the kind folks at Servant Books—particularly Cindy Cavnar—were willing to take a flier on me solely on Mike's good word. To the other victimless criminals who meet at the Sharpedge Creekhouse in Crafton, Pennsylvania, every third Thursday of the month for talk and libations, you can't be blamed, but I'm holding you responsible.

To the bishops who taught me to live as if the kingdom is coming, that nothing is impossible with God and that the good life is waiting in joyful hope, thank you for your guidance and friendship. To the nuns who put up with me and to a thousand priests—from my first pastor to the priest who suffers with me at Pirates games—thank you for showing me what vocation means.

The stories in this book come out of a lifetime of experiences that have taught me that God's great gifts to us are the people who touch our lives. Friends and family, cousins and classmates too many to count, a woman of a certain age, a flight attendant on a plane and a guy who sold me Chuckles—thank you all. And Matt and Maggie, Emily, John's dad and, in particular, Mark, thank you for your heroism.

And to my spouse, Cindy. She shines like Dante's Beatrice.

.

.

.

.

.

.

{The Virtues}

While halfway through the journey of our life
I found myself lost in a darkened forest,
for I had wandered off from the straight path.

How I entered there I cannot truly say,
I had become so sleepy at the moment
when I first strayed, leaving the path of truth.

—Dante Alighieri, *The Divine Comedy*[1]

It wasn't a dark wood. It was a ten-year-old Toyota with an odometer that had cracked 160,000 miles. The transmission had started talking to me, and the "Check Engine" light had been burning bright for months.

The guy at the oil change express had just warned me that the tires wouldn't pass Pennsylvania state inspection. I could tell by the look on his face that he figured I ought to give it a wash one of these days as well. But the radio still worked, pulling in an oldies station that served as background noise while I chewed up miles on the parkway.

I was in an after-work-on-Tuesday kind of mood, when the new week has lost its novelty and Friday is nothing but a dim hope. I was listening to the oldies station, because anything newer just reminds me of a music video instead of a slice of life. The Beatles' 1964 release of the Isley Brothers' "Twist and Shout" crackled out of the radio, courtesy of an antenna with more bends in it than a country road. I didn't care. Even with static it's still rock and roll.

As I listened to the late John Lennon knock it out of the park, I slipped into the Wayback Machine. It was the summer after my sophomore year in high school. I was a fifteen-year-old kid at a "Record Hop" at North Eastham, Cape Cod, around mid-August. They played forty-fives off an old record player for the summer kids at a town hall that had no practical purpose immediately after Labor Day. If not for the summer folks, the Cape back then would have been nothing but dunes, crabs and saltwater.

The guy running the show put on the Beatles' "Twist and Shout." Fifteen seconds into it all the kids had stopped dancing and were singing the song at the top of their lungs. When it was over everybody laughed and clapped.

Now this overweight guy with gray hair and a bald spot in back started coughing before he could get to the chorus. But he still laughed when it was over.

Time Bandit

Time. It yanks us through history before we even know we are in it. One moment I'm fancy free at a dance with buddies I am convinced I'll have for the rest of my days. And then I'm a thousand miles and decades away, an out-of-shape old geezer heading home after putting in another eight hours. And the string connecting it is a song John Lennon recorded in 1963 on a day when he had a terrible cold, which is what made those lyrics so raspy.

Climbing out of the Wayback Machine and sitting behind the wheel of my bucket of bolts, I wondered about the kind of kid I was and the kind of guy I had become. And I wondered about the kind of guy I wanted to be—maybe the kind of guy we all want to be.

But Dante found himself in a dark wood after he had "wandered off from the straight path." It was the beginning of his journey, his *Divine Comedy*. Along the way he was blocked by the Leopard, representing fraud; the Lion, symbolizing violence; and the She-wolf, which meant, well, as the old moralists used to say, "concupiscence"- -a Catholic word that we use for over-the top sexual temptations because we don't like to come out and say "over-the top sexual temptations." Though if the truth be told, "concupiscence" sounds dirtier.

Dante's literary pilgrimage—composed in the early fourteenth century and considered one of the "Great Books" of Western culture—was a guided tour through hell, purgatory and heaven. Our pilgrimage is usually not so dramatic, though we often find ourselves in that dark wood. It's an Everyman kind of feeling that for me seems to burp up to the surface in a car drive home after a rough day or on a bar stool in a town far from home. There are a lot of ways to describe it—it can be as simple as ennui or as complicated as that "quiet desperation" the philosopher described as a man's lot in life. But I prefer to call it the "what-the-hells," as in "What the hell am I doing with my life?"

Scripture tells us that the just man sins seven times a day. I think the just man gets a case of "what-the-hells" at least as often. It's wondering why I do what I do and why I can't be the person I would like to be. It has nothing to do with a lack of, or certainly an abundance of, money, power or sex—the great triumvirate of our sins and ambitions. It's more like slipping away from a fundamental purpose and not being able to get back. It's not about how I make a living but how I live. It's falling into the trap described by that heady theologian "Broadway Joe" Namath to the TV cameras over a game of eight ball back in the 1960s: He was just trying to get by. It's reaching a point, which I seem to reach seven times a day, where I know I can be better but have lost the ability—or the energy—to do so. Or even to figure out how.

When the rubber hits the road, what we really want out of our lives is happiness. Not three-beer happiness, I-got-a-raise happiness or the-Steelers-made-the-playoffs happiness but that quiet contentment that comes with living a good life. It's not created by the circumstances of our lives, but rather it is the circumstances of our living. It's how we walk the road, how we live the pilgrimage.

A Little Scripture

We all remember the story of the rich young man. It is mentioned in similar form in Matthew, Mark and Luke. In the Gospel of Luke (18:18–30), the rich young man is identified as an official. Jesus has just told the disciples not to prevent children from crowding around him: "Whoever does not receive the kingdom of God like a child shall not enter it" (18:17). As if on cue, a rich man approaches Jesus and asks him what he must do to gain eternal life.

Jesus replies that the man already knows the answer to that

question: Keep the commandments. The rich man replies that he has done all of that from his youth. He presses Jesus, like a gambler wanting the sure thing. What more can I do? What will guarantee eternal life?

It's easy to imagine Jesus pausing for a moment and reading the man's soul. A fellow who confesses to keeping the commandments perfectly might not have quite the right impression of himself. So Jesus responds that if keeping the commandments is not enough, here's what you need to do: Sell all you have, give it to the poor and come follow me.

You can almost hear the music going flat in the background. Like the old rock song from Meatloaf, the rich fellow thought he could do anything for love, but he couldn't do that.

Jesus watches him walk away and remarks to his disciples, "How hard it is for those who have riches to enter the kingdom of God!" (18:24). To which the disciples respond, "Then who can be saved?" And Jesus gives an answer that just about sums up Scripture: "What is impossible with men is possible with God" (18:27).

Which gives me a lot of hope.

The thing that always strikes me is that Luke, Matthew and Mark tell us that the rich official, or the rich young man, walked away sad because he had a lot of stuff. The usual explanation is that he fell short: He couldn't bear to part with his riches. But I always thought that he was sad for a deeper reason. He wasn't being offered an impossible task: He knew he could do it. He could give it all away; he could live the great life, starting right then and there. But he decided not to.

So he was sad not because he couldn't do it but because he could. He had pressed Jesus for an answer, and Jesus had told him what he could do to make the run for sanctity. And he gave the Meatloaf response.

Benign Mediocrity

When given the option for greatness in life, it's easy to opt out time and time again, until it becomes a habit. And it has nothing to do with preferring money or power or sex. It has to do with a more subtle temptation: benign mediocrity. It's more comfortable to be ordinary than a saint. Or at least that's what it is comfortable to believe.

A lot of our little battles in Dante's dark wood are created not just because we choose sin but because we avoid good. Good seems too hard; mediocrity seems so easy. We look at what we admire in others and decide we just don't measure up, without realizing that the key to understanding the great life is that it is not just how we are created to live but the way we want to live. Dante put it right:

> How I entered there I cannot truly say,
>   I had become so sleepy at the moment
>   when I first strayed, leaving the path of truth.

And "leaving the path of truth" is so easy to do on the pilgrimage. It's not always a matter of some great sin, some great wrong that yanks us off the path. It's usually just becoming "so sleepy" that we lose our place, as in a book we don't earmark for the next time we pick it up.

When I wore a younger man's clothes, I had a little patter to get the ladies giggling. I'd explain to them that the key to understanding men is that none of us have layers. It was my "Shallow Man" theory, meaning, what you see is what you get. Women make the mistake of looking for depth in men when there is none, I'd tell them.

"What are men really thinking?" a lady would ask.

And my answer would be: "Nothing. Nothing at all."

It got the laughs because it fit every silly caricature of men, from Curly of the Three Stooges to Dagwood Bumstead. And it is absolute nonsense. As Pascal wrote, "Man is infinitely more than man."[2]

I know a lot about the collected works of Oliver Hardy but not much at all about the English novelist Thomas Hardy, except that he abandoned novels to write poetry. The explanation I read, described ironically by the novelist Stephen King, is that "fiction's goals were forever beyond his reach, that the job was an exercise in futility. 'Compared to the dullest human being actually walking about on the face of the earth and casting his shadow there,' Hardy supposedly said, 'the most brilliantly drawn character in a novel is but a bag of bones.'"[3]

Hamlet and Ahab have nothing on a bus driver or a bank teller. Not when it comes to the richness and complexity of what we think, feel, believe and experience at any given moment of our lives. Nope. There's no such thing as the shallow man, no matter how shallow he might behave on occasion. Granted, when I'm eating a bologna, egg and cheese sandwich—called a "Pittsburgh Steak Hoagie" at a tavern I frequent—while channel-surfing for *The Simpsons* reruns, I'm not exactly King Lear. But I'm also not a bag of bones. None of us are.

Wisdom From an "Old Feller"
Dredging the mall for the detritus of the consumer culture for male clothing is not usually my idea of a good time, which is why

I dress the way I do. But when my wife decides that the ten-year-old shirts are old enough, she insists on my presence. So I go.

On one of those trips to the mall, I begged off for a few-minute break from the sensory overload of trying to pick out a shirt from a stack of fifty and escaped to the sunlight. I sat down on one of the metal benches outside, and an old feller sauntered by and asked if I had room to spare. I always have room to spare for an old feller.

He was dressed in Early Retirement—a pair of striped shorts, white T-shirt, black socks and sneakers off the clearance rack of a department store. He was a mall walker, putting his time in not so much for the exercise as for something to do. He sat down not for a break but because I looked like a guy who would listen and not interrupt. He was right.

The wife had died before him, which always leaves a man bewildered. It's like the natural order of things is disrupted. He was living alone, but his daughter was nearby, and she stopped by four or five times a week. He made it sound like an imposition rather than a blessing.

The old feller lived on a little bit of a pension, from a steel mill job that went belly-up before he was done with it, and Social Security, which got him grumbling about the government and the Republicans. He had a grandkid, and I got the impression that a son-in-law was not part of the story.

We sipped some coffee and surreptitiously eyeballed a pretty young thing walking by.

"You know what keeps a man going?" he asked me.

Thinking I'm the straight man in this one, I responded, "Guilt, debt and responsibility."

"Where'd you get that bit of philosophy?"

"From a comic strip," I admitted.

"You know what I'd do if I had fifteen thousand bucks?" he said, picking out a number that to him was as impossible to imagine as a million bucks. "I'd go to Alaska. I was there in the military back when I was a kid. I'd go back in a second."

I think his dream of Alaska was more focused on youth than the frozen tundra. There's always a good time to be had back then, whether we're an old feller walking the mall or a twenty-six-year-old pining over a lost love from senior year in high school.

One thing that can make us old fast is thinking that we are getting old. Mitch Robbins, the Billy Crystal character in the movie *City Slickers*, in the throes of middle-age angst, lamented the potbelly, the surgeries, the hearing loss, till finally "you and the wife retire to Fort Lauderdale, you start eating dinner at two, lunch around ten, breakfast the night before. And you spend most of your time wandering around malls looking for the ultimate in soft yogurt and muttering, 'How come the kids don't call?'"

"And one man in his time plays many parts," I thought, scrounging a line from an otherwise wasted college education. Shakespeare described the stages of a man's life, from infancy to its final moments. He concluded:

> ...Last scene of all,
> That ends this strange eventful history,
> Is second childishness and mere oblivion,
> Sans teeth, sans eyes, sans taste, sans everything.[4]

Shakespeare wrote that for laughs. We don't laugh much when we read it today.

The old feller got up and did a little stretch. He'd buy a lottery ticket that afternoon, he said. He was feeling lucky. One big hit, and it was off to Alaska.

"You know what keeps a man going?" he asked again.

Still expecting a punch line, I answered, "Alaska?"

"Nope. It's what the nuns told us—faith, hope and love. Most of all love."

"I think Saint Paul said that. Lennon said that too," I admitted.

"The Commie?"

"No. The Beatle. All you need is love."

Then I wished him good luck on the lottery. And good luck on life.

Wisdom From Saint Paul

When Saint Paul saw that "the time of my departure has come," he wrote to Timothy, "I have fought the good fight, I have finished the race, I have kept the faith" (2 Timothy 4:6–7).

Saint Paul speaks well to men:

> Owe no one anything, except to love one another; for he who loves his neighbor has fulfilled the law. The commandments, "You shall not commit adultery, You shall not kill, You shall not steal, You shall not covet," and any other commandments, are summed up in this sentence, "You shall love your neighbor as yourself." Love does no wrong to a neighbor; therefore, love is the fulfilling of the law. (Romans 13:8–10)

What Paul is discussing for us here is what we call virtue. The nuns spoke of the theological virtues—faith, hope and love. And the cardinal virtues, the moral virtues that are faith, hope and love lived: prudence, justice, fortitude and temperance. All these virtues Paul has defined for us in Romans. He has defined for us how we are to live, answering that eternal question of men: "What the hell am I doing with my life?"

Which was the point Jesus made to the rich young man.

Virtue is classically defined as the habit of performing actions for good. These virtues we either naturally gain and acquire by the repetition of good acts (the cardinal virtues) or come to through the grace of God (the theological virtues). The virtues are how we are meant to live. They are what we admire in others and hope to find in ourselves, if only through a mirror darkly.

Many of us have spent years trying to convince ourselves that life based on the virtues is too hard, involving more change than any one person can accomplish. But with grace, the sacraments and the "repetition of good acts," this great life—a life for which we all strive—is not only attainable but easier than the opposite.

It's said that the natives of Rome sometimes feel oppressed by the city's very history. It's hard to think of yourself as a unique child of God in a city where a thousand-year-old piece of sculpture is the new stuff. You can get lost in time that way. Time becomes the enemy; history, a sad tale from our early memories to the dust that we will most surely become—"sans teeth, sans eyes, sans taste, sans everything."

But as Pope Benedict XVI once explained, we can never get lost in history, never get lost in time, if we understand our simple task: "Be seeds of holiness scattered by the handful in the furrows of history."[5] Even John Lennon never managed a lyric like that.

So the journey begins.

Lord, let me live each day with the knowledge that I mean something. I have work to do in this life, more to accomplish than I will ever know, if I keep your commandments and live by the virtues you have given through your grace and the virtues I practice from morning until the last light of evening. Let me spend my waking hours seeking an example, finding an example, being an example. And give me faith to believe, hope to bear and love to endure. Amen.

·

·

·

·

·

·

PART ONE

{The Cardinal Virtues}

The cardinal virtues of prudence, justice, temperance and fortitude form the basics of a virtuous life. They form the way that we look at the world and the way we act in the world. They are what we admire in others and try to cultivate in ourselves.

The cardinal virtues, in the classical sense, are the summation of a morally good character. We learn these virtues as we practice them.

.
.
.
.
.
.

CHAPTER ONE

{ Prudence }

Prudence: the virtue of using intellect and conscience to search out the true good in every circumstance and to choose the morally licit means of achieving that good. It is the virtue of divorcing personal desire from the judgment of whether an act is right or wrong. It is seeing truth and pursuing it. Prudence is reason and discernment made in kindness and truth.

Dave Swallow expected a catastrophe to occur when the clock would strike the New Year on January 1, 2000. He wanted to be prepared. And he was prepared as no Boy Scout ever dreamed.

Dave was from Fort Wayne, Indiana. His story was told in a late September 1999 issue of *The Fort Wayne News Sentinel*, just a few months before the second millennium ground to a halt. He was caught up in the Y2K end-times scare.

We were warned that as the curtains closed on the twentieth century, all hell would break loose. With computers running our lives as well as our cars, and with all of them programmed only through the year 1999, everything subject to their electronic razzle-dazzle would fizzle out like a flat beer. Planes wouldn't fly, the power company would collapse, coffee makers would quit—really apocalyptic stuff.

The Y2K scare created its own little boom in the waning months of the second millennium, based on a mixture of theological millennialism and pseudoscientific harum-scarum. It created a subculture in America, with suckers waiting to get soaked and the soakers waiting for the suckers.

Dave lived by himself in a pleasant enough middle-class home in Middle America. It was a home with a lot of room to spare for just one guy. That's the space Dave converted into a Y2K storehouse that would make a paranoiac snug and smug. He was prepared for a Cormac McCarthy novel. If the end of civilization was coming after the first New Year's kiss, Dave was not going to be caught short on the necessities.

According to the newspaper story, Dave had crammed his house with, among other things, more than 1,000 cans of food, 18 boxes of Band-Aids, at least a ton of charcoal briquettes, 1,500 pounds of propane, shelf after shelf of toilet paper, 9,500 plastic cups, 268 rolls of paper towels, a mountain of disposable razor blades, gallons of mouthwash and 216 cases of beer—all the flotsam and jetsam of modern American life crammed into one little home on a corner at a busy intersection.

Dave was on a trip with a friend the summer of 1999. They had just enjoyed a solid Midwest breakfast together. As they walked back to his truck, Dave suddenly keeled over. He was as dead as a doornail before he hit the ground, victim of a heart attack at the age of fifty-three. Which is a reminder that the old rock-song warning "Don't stop thinking about tomorrow" can be overstated.

Dave needed a little touch of prudence.

Dear Prudence

Prudence has taken on a certain meaning in our times different from the classical sense. Contemporary conversation defines prudence as an older aunt in comfortable shoes making choices that are so sensible that they ooze boredom. The word then gets tossed together with prudery, and that aunt takes on a disdainful pucker while she frets about hemlines and pick up lines.

Prudence is actually a very straightforward guy's virtue. It means living in the truth, not as a self-righteous jerk but as a guy who wants to look at himself in the mirror every morning without fearing that he's sold out. Prudence doesn't mean living on a prudish straight and narrow with visors on, but it does mean living in society and culture by thought-out, reasoned principles that don't fall prey to conventional wisdom. A prudent man looks for truth, finds truth and lives truth. No matter where it leads him.

It's easier said than done, my friends. It can even make watching football a challenge.

I'm thinking back to one of the most well-known moments in the history of the Super Bowl, and I'm not referring to David Tyree gluing a pass from Eli Manning to the side of his helmet to set up the Giants' upset of the New England Patriots in 2008. I'm referring instead to singer Justin Timberlake's tearing off part of Janet Jackson's outfit during their halftime songfest at the 2004 Super Bowl. This momentarily revealed Ms. Jackson's breast, on live network television, to a legion of football fans who had not sensibly retreated to the kitchen for beer and pizza during the game's intermission.

Mr. Timberlake explained—in a line that came perilously close to the late Ron Ziegler's claim that certain Watergate explanations from the Nixon White House were "no longer operative"—that a "wardrobe malfunction" caused the overexposure. Ms. Jackson later admitted it was a prearranged malfunction. Which seemed obvious, as Mr. Timberlake crooned these immortal lines just before tearing her outfit: "I'll have you naked by the end of this song."

The producers of the halftime show issued the ubiquitous nonapologetic apology for tastelessness: "We apologize to anyone who was offended." Which implies, of course, that the offense was merely in the perception, not in the act itself. A coward's apology if there ever was one. Ms. Jackson and Mr. Timberlake's little show was tastelessness forced on an unsuspecting audience that included a lot of children.

Bad taste has become virtually epidemic in American culture. Parameters are now defined by the unrestrained libido of a male high school sophomore and the sense of humor of a six-year-old enchanted by scatological jokes. If you watch television it can seem that the most highly paid, creative minds in America offer a celebration of our culture centered on underwear fetishes, sex and intestinal gas, in no particular order.

We see an intentional coarsening of our culture, time and time again proving that we have defined deviancy down. One former television executive was arguing after the wardrobe malfunction at the Super Bowl that this was a tempest in a teapot. "After all," he said, "it's not like child pornography or... uh, uh, uh..." He was stuck. Other than blatant child pornography, he was hard pressed to define what exactly we should consider offensive anymore on television. That's the sinister aspect of all this. The culture keeps defining deviancy down, and after a while there's nothing left to define as deviant—including child pornography.

At some point the prudent man has to make choices.

Prudent Saints

Cradle Catholics grew up with the saints. At least they did when I was growing up, just prior to electricity and running water. Converts might think that this familiarity with the saints was a good thing, but it had its drawbacks. Bad enough when your mother asked why you couldn't be more like your brother, your cousin or that annoying kid with the perfect grades right up the street. We also got, "Why can't you be more like Saint Francis of Assisi?"

But somewhere along the line the saints got sidetracked in our lives, or at least in my life. Perhaps the good sisters idealized them so much that I forgot that they were real flesh-and-blood people. But the older I get the smarter those good sisters look, and I've gone to school again on the saints.

Bear with me for a brief history lesson.

In the sixteenth century the testosterone level of King Henry VIII led to the near destruction of Catholicism in England. Henry moved from wife to wife, hoping to sire a male heir, and ended up in schism from the Church. Saint Thomas More faced martyrdom under Henry.

But it was really under Henry's daughter Elizabeth I that England codified the first modern police state aimed specifically at eliminating Catholics and their priests. The Catholic faith, which had been at the heart of English life at the beginning of the sixteenth century, nearly disappeared in a wave of persecution and harassment from the government and its spy network. By the 1570s any observer of the English Catholic scene would have agreed that the Church was dying.

It was death by a thousand cuts, caused by Elizabeth's policy of isolating the Catholic community, denying it priests to celebrate the sacraments and imposing a host of fines and humiliations that left it leaderless and apathetic. For all intents and purposes, Catholicism in England had become criminal.

But a backlash was coming. A devoted group of young Catholic men were considering a mission to their own land, even if it meant torture and death upon capture by the authorities. Many would cross the channel to Europe to study for the priesthood, vowing to return to invigorate and renew the Catholic faithful of England. One of them wrote in the late 1570s:

> Listen to our heavenly Father asking back his talents with usury; listen to the Church, the mother that bore us and nursed us, imploring our help; listen to the pitiful cries of our neighbours in danger of spiritual starvation; listen to the howling of the wolves that are spoiling the flock. The glory of your Father, the preservation of your mother, your own salvation, the safety of your brethren, are in jeopardy, and you can stand idle?...[S]leep not while the enemy watches; play not while he devours his prey; relax not in idleness and vanity while he is dabbling in your brother's blood![1]

That was straight from the pen of a youthful Edmund Campion.

A Champion of Truth

As a brilliant young student at Oxford, Campion had caught the eye of Queen Elizabeth, and it appeared he was on the path to glory: a high rank in the Church of England and perhaps a sterling career in government or law. In 1568 Campion was ordained to the Church of England, a first step on this path.

But Edmund's conscience intervened. Within four years the young man with an established reputation as a scholar and writer, and with an assured position in the new Church hierarchy, threw it all away. He would become a Catholic priest and commit himself to rejuvenating the Catholics of England as a member of the newly founded Jesuit order.

In 1580 Father Campion returned to England. He was told to serve the Catholic faithful there and have nothing to do with battling those who persecuted the Church. And his arrival was instantly invigorating. He created "buzz," this bright young star, both within the Catholic community and in government circles that feared these dedicated Catholics returning to their homeland. They particularly feared this "one above the rest notorious for impudency and audacity, named Campion."[2]

The life of these new missionaries could not have been more difficult. They hid from house to house, celebrating clandestine Masses, while spies were constantly tracking their movements, the law always on their heels. Catholic homes included "priest holes," small openings behind walls into which a priest could be stuffed at a moment's notice when the law came banging at the door. To this day restoration workers in old English Catholic homes stumble across sixteenth-century hiding places that had been forgotten to time.

But Father Campion longed to do battle. In a letter to government officials, he begged for the opportunity to defend the faith in order "to win you to heaven, or to die upon your pikes."[3]

To Catholics it was a stirring call to hope; to the government it was a war cry, and Campion's was a voice to be silenced at all costs. Finally he was caught, uncovered when a local authority found lose plaster in a Catholic home and took a crowbar to it.

Taken to London under armed escort, Campion went to trial four months later, charged in a trumped-up plot of mass conspiracy to murder. It was a calculated attempt by the government to avoid any intellectual or theological arguments with the learned Campion. But who knows if he could have responded? He had been tortured on the rack while confined to the Tower, so much so that at his trial he was unable to raise his hands to take an oath.

The results were a foregone conclusion. Campion was found guilty. Led from the Tower along the muddy streets of London in a driving rain, he was hanged, drawn and quartered before the assembled crowds. He was forty-one years old. He was canonized as a martyr for the faith on October 25, 1970.

Saint Edmund, and many of his fellow martyrs in sixteenth- and seventeenth-century England, saw a Catholic faithful that had been beaten down by a propaganda machine that painted Catholics and the Catholic Church as the very enemies of enlightened English culture. And that's what they wanted to answer, at the risk of their lives. They did it for one reason: to save souls. They had to stand up for truth, no matter the cost.

They were prudent.

Contrapasso *With Dante*

When I was a kid I had fantasies of being a basketball player. And I mean fantasies. I was the shortest kid in class—girls included—and would have been one of the shortest in the class behind me at Christ the King School in Yonkers, New York. But I ate and drank basketball.

Day in and day out, winter, spring, summer or fall, I was out there shooting baskets. A right-hander, I'd practice for at least one day a week using only my left hand. I'd shoot shot after shot, dribble forward, backward, side to side. Layups, hook shots, set shots and free throws—I'd shoot twenty-five of each at a time. As a result of all that work, I almost reached average, which was pretty good for a kid who hadn't hit sixty inches in height by eighth grade.

Basketball became such an obsession that I would actually dream of it. And the dream was always the same, like that college dream of showing up for a final in a class you had forgotten to take. I would be on the court, right under the basket. Everybody else would be all the way up at the other end. They would throw a pass down to me, and there I would be, all alone, looking at a simple layup. I'd shoot it as I had practiced a million times before in my driveway, and the ball would bounce off the rim, back into my hands. I'd shoot it again and bang it off the backboard. A third shot would miss, and desperate, I'd take a final shot before being enveloped by a horde of defenders. And miss again. Four of the easiest shots in the world, and I couldn't put it in the basket. I'd wake up with the sweats, and decades later I can remember that sense of helplessness.

I didn't realize that I was dreaming Dante's *Inferno*. In the *Divine Comedy* Dante punishes sinners by *contrapasso*. The punishment mirrors—or counterbalances—the sin committed in life. As Charles Dickens put it in *The Christmas Carol*, "we wear the chains we forged in life." My little basketball hell was standing under the basket with a wide-open shot and missing it for all eternity.

Just outside the first circle of hell, Dante positions those who "lived / a life worthy of neither blame nor praise."[4] These souls are so unreflective, so lacking in passion, that neither heaven nor hell will accept them. They spent their lives refusing to take any sides, to mount any battles, to live for any cause. Not only did they fail to search for truth, but they refused to recognize its existence. Their lives are testaments to benign mediocrity.

Dante describes the monster Geryon, the personification of fraud:

> His face was the face of any honest man,
> it shone with such a look of benediction;
> and all the rest of him was serpentine.[5]

Such are the opposite of prudent men. They refuse to seek out the truthful, and their own desires—even if those desires are to spend a lifetime lying low—are their only true quest. Dante condemns them *contrapasso* to an eternity of running back and forth, chasing a banner they will never catch.

Prudent men are those willing to live and die by truth, particularly in the overpowering and overwhelming world of contemporary culture, where deviancy is defined ever downward. They refuse to live in the mire of a benign mediocrity. Prudent men are stand-up guys when the rest of the world is sitting down.

A Little Scripture

Dante describes one poor wretch among those who make up that babble of benign mediocrity chasing banners for all eternity. He calls him "the coward who had made the great refusal." We meet him in the Gospels.

Matthew tells us that after Jesus was betrayed, the Sanhedrin arraigned him before Pilate, the Roman procurator. They wanted him dead, and only a conviction by the Roman authorities could accomplish that. He was charged with plotting to become the "King of the Jews," which meant his business was insurrection. Roman justice would be swift and merciless if he was convicted.

Pilate asks Jesus, "Are you the King of the Jews?" (Matthew 27:11). We can imagine him sounding almost bored. In the Gospel of John, Jesus answers, "You say that I am a king. For this I was born, and for this I have come into the world, to bear witness to the truth. Every one who is of the truth hears my voice" (John 18:37).

"What is truth?" Pilate answers for two thousand years of a cynical humanity (John 18:38).

The rest of the story is straightforward. Pilate has Jesus scourged and claims he finds no guilt in the man—at least not enough to have him crucified. But the crowd wants blood and even refuses Pilate's offer to free Jesus, calling instead for the freedom of the troublemaker Barabbas. Pilate's wife warns him, "Have nothing to do with that righteous man, for I have suffered much over him today in a dream" (Matthew 27:19).

Pilate turns from Truth. The innocent man will die, he decides, if only to keep the peace. Seems like a small price to pay.

Pilate makes one last dramatic gesture, perhaps to clear his conscience but more likely an act of near-perfect cynicism. Calling for a bowl of water, he washes his hands in front of the crowd and declares, "I am innocent of this righteous man's blood. See to it yourselves" (Matthew 27:24). And forevermore he will be "the coward who had made the great refusal." Because he couldn't recognize Truth standing right in front of him.

Speaking of Truth

After four decades of driving, I received my first traffic ticket courtesy of a Pennsylvania state trooper. Sure, I had gotten a few parking tickets, but they were back in my salad days in New York, for violating the "alternate side of the street" parking restrictions. You needed a Harvard law degree to understand those rules, so those tickets don't count. And anyway, they weren't moving violations.

My crime was exceeding an alleged fifty-five-mile-per-hour speed limit on a miniscule stretch of a road that was sixty-five miles per hour before and after. You know where this is going. When the cop wrote out the ticket, it was rationalization time.

Like every guy in the joint, I was convinced I was an innocent man, a victim of circumstances. The next day I checked the road signs, checked where the lower speed limit began and where it ended. And I was guilty as sin. No doubt singing along with an old Beatles' tune on the radio at the time, I had breezed through the restricted zone well over the speed limit. I could claim I never saw the signs, wrapped up in the moment of "Hey Jude." But the truth was plain to see, no matter whether I saw it or not. And that's pretty much a fact of life for all of us.

When Frank Conroy, jazz pianist and author of the award-winning "Stop-Time," died in 2005, there was a long profile of him by James Salter in the Sunday *New York Times* book review section. Conroy was a legend among American writers, head of the Iowa Writers' Workshop at the University of Iowa for eighteen years. He died at the age of sixty-nine—cancer.

Salter told this story about Conroy:

> Objectivity came up more than once and the existence of truth, or God's truth, as Frank called it. No one could know that, the complete truth. It was too vast and complex. "All we know is what we think we know," he said; there was really no such thing as truth or fact. He told me he had written that his mother and stepfather had gone to Cuba to buy a piano or something—actually it was for her to have an abortion. But what he wrote was what he thought was true. "For me it was true," he said.[6]

If Salter's recollection is correct, in one sense old Frank Conroy was right. There's a difference between God's truth and what can pass for our phony ideas of truth. But Salter seems to imply that Conroy's great insight is that truth is simply what we think, no matter what the reality might be. Because the truth itself—God's truth—can't be known. Which is downright silly.

Conroy lost an innocent sibling, no matter what he believed, no matter what he wrote. Truth exists, and it can be known. God's truth exists, and it can be known. For if God's truth can't be known or understood, then there is no truth at all. And God becomes pointless in our lives. It is that kind of thinking that is at the root of contemporary humanity's despair.

Nothing new here, of course. Thomas Aquinas described the evident source of truth:

> What God's Son has told me, take for truth I do;
> Truth Himself speaks truly or there's nothing true.[7]

A Stranger in a Strange Land

There are times in life when we are hit with change, fundamental change. There are the obvious moments, of course: the principal shaking your hand for the first time because he knows he will never see you again as you accept your high school diploma; the priest pronouncing you married; the doctor saying, "It's a girl!"

But there are the less obvious moments or at least those moments obvious to you if not to everyone around you. Yet they still mean things have changed fundamentally and won't ever be the same. Maybe it's the first time your knee hurts when you try to run full speed or when the Three Stooges just don't seem as funny as they did before.

My day of reckoning was a softball game in my early thirties. I was playing right field when a fly ball was hit my way, curving toward the foul line. I started to run for it.

There's a feeling that anyone who has ever played the outfield knows. It's an actual physical sensation that you are going to catch the ball, as if the brain has done the geometry of the angles and the physics of your speed and is letting you know everything is fine. It had never failed me in decades of playing. I stretched out my glove, and I knew the ball would be there. And it wasn't. I was a half step short. I stood there staring at my glove as if it had done something wrong.

And then I knew. I knew it in my soul before my brain realized it. I had started to get old.

I was sitting at a high school graduation a number of years ago next to an older couple. The valedictorian was giving a speech laced with references to *Forrest Gump*, at the time a hugely popular movie with Tom Hanks playing a dim-witted savant. It became obvious that the older couple was without a clue. Not having been aware of the phenomenon of *Forrest Gump*, all the allusions to the movie—like life being a box of chocolates—were incomprehensible to them. The valedictorian's speech might as well have been in Portuguese.

My time will come, if it is not already here. I have no idea what the top songs are today, have no desire to see the movies that are consistently grabbing the coveted eighteen to-thirty-five-year-old market and wear essentially the same style of clothes that I wore twenty years ago. Every joke I know I heard no later than my senior year in college.

The final indignity is realizing that there is an entire nostalgia industry based on cultural detritus accumulated twenty-five years after I was born. Adults are fondly recalling things from their childhood that are meaningless to me because I was grown up when they were kids.

I'm a stranger in a strange land.

There is a lesson in all this. Perhaps it is a reminder that the ephemeral is really ephemeral. After all, the older couple clueless about *Forrest Gump* seemed none the worse for that, and what possible difference could it make today? We invest a great deal in the passing parade, the bread and circuses of our lives. Maybe prudence also means a better understanding that there are things worth knowing about and many things not worth knowing about. Wisdom is knowing the difference.

Shopping for Truth?

As anyone could tell from my lack of sartorial splendor, I'm not exactly a clothes hound. And the usual baubles that might appeal to your normal American male—power tools, golf clubs and fishing gear—hold no attraction for me. Tools are a mystery, golf numbers eight on my personal list of the seven deadly sins, and fishing is about as electrifying to me as a fabric store to an eight-year-old boy.

But I go shopping because my wife enjoys going from time to time, and I like being with my wife. It makes for a nice afternoon together, and if I don't pout and whine, she lets me get junk food at the end of the day. Every man has his price, and mine is a slice of greasy pepperoni pizza.

So we were out shopping, taking a little break to watch the world go by. I commenced with the speech.

"You know, the kids all look the same. Throw the teenage girls in a sack, and I could still describe any one of them: blonde-streaked hair, white shirt with the navel peeking out like a third eye, low-slung, hip-hugging jeans and clunky, oversized shoes," I harrumphed.

"And then there are the guys: backward baseball cap, oversized pro basketball shirt and sneakers. And those baggy short pants that go to the mid-calf—or are they long pants that are too short?—with a sag in the crotch that gives them enough room to hide a watermelon between the knees."

"Wait till we get home, old man," she said.

Once there she pulled out a photo album that my mother had put together, documenting my life and hard times from bare-bottomed infancy to college graduation day. The wife thumbed through, stopped at a particular page and handed it to me.

"Take a look," she said.

There I was with my old buddy Ed, in a shot taken at Cape Cod the summer of my fifteenth year. I had to admit, I was very cool. I was dressed in what we called a pea coat—a woolen navy blue jacket—with the cuffs unbuttoned, cut-off shorts that I had trimmed from old jeans and a pair of sneakers *sans* socks. A shock of unruly blonde hair fell over one eye, as I looked into the camera with an insouciant grin.

"You should have known me then," I said with a sly chuckle.

She said, "Take a look at your buddy."

Ed was dressed in a pea coat with the cuffs unbuttoned, cut-off shorts that he had trimmed from old jeans and a pair of sneakers *sans* socks. A shock of unruly red hair fell over one eye, as he looked into the camera with an insouciant grin.

So it goes.

Life is a search for a lot of things, often contradictory. We try to understand who we are as living, breathing individuals; yet we latch on to the crowd to blend in as best we can to an amorphous definition of humanity. We proclaim the freedom of our intellects but get most of our ideas secondhand from the daily bombardment of the cultural propaganda machine.

Pope John Paul II had it right. He viewed the status of contemporary man and saw the great cause of our fear and anxiety in the struggle to find out who we are and to define our lives. The twentieth century gave us a lot of bad answers to those fundamental questions. Among other things it offered race, sex, gender, nation, economic class and consumerism as the answer. The Holy Father said that the answer is right in front of us. It is Christ. In him we find who we are and what our life means. We find Truth.

Prudence is recognizing that truth and living by it. Even when we are shopping.

And in the End

Going to a small Catholic high school, I thought I had a shot at the basketball team. But I didn't make the freshman team. In sophomore year I didn't make the cut for the junior varsity. Ditto junior year.

But I kept honing my skills with intramural ball and my parish CYO league. Like a ballplayer in Triple-A who could never cut it in the majors, I did pretty well in these games, playing to no crowds in endless shirts-and-skins games.

But the dreams end at some point. I had my final failure trying out for varsity senior year—thanks, but no thanks. Our high school team fared pretty well in the Catholic league that year, but I watched the games from the bleachers. Another desultory year of intramural ball, and I was done.

Our yearbook, passed out just before graduation, included a little "biography" under each senior's picture. I remember standing in the school hallway getting my first read of the yearbook staff's summation of my life. Along with a quite reasonably short listing of my academic achievements and a notice of the college I would be attending, I was described as a "successful foul shooter." It might sound like chump change, but I appreciated it.

The reporter who did the Dave Swallow story gave him the benefit of the doubt. He described Dave as kind of a loner but not the kind who becomes the Tapioca Killer or a stalker of late-night talk-show hosts.

Dave had centered his life for many years around his mother. They would do almost everything together. A special treat was looking for small town eateries where they enjoyed their dinner together, a middle-aged single man with his elderly mother.

When his mother's health began to go in her eighties, it was Dave who took care of her. When she died Dave mourned deeply. At some point soon after he buried her, the Y2K obsession took hold.

The reporter wondered if Dave's stash, while obsessive, was not self-centered. No one knows for sure, but maybe there was a method in his madness. If the Y2K catastrophe struck, Dave would be able to make everything OK. The attorney handling Dave's estate hoped that he was storing stuff so that he could set up a soup kitchen to take care of his neighbors after the ball dropped.

I like to think that maybe Dave was a prudent man after all.

.

.

.

.

.

.

CHAPTER TWO

{Fortitude}

Fortitude is the virtue of living true to the faith in good times and bad. It's not meek acceptance but strength to carry on. In the classic definition fortitude means firmness in times of difficulty and constancy in the pursuit of the good. With fortitude we face the fearful and live each day in hope. It is Christian courage lived.

I'm a displaced New York Mets fan, living in Pennsylvania. At the beginning of the season a few years back, I was chatting it up with an acquaintance when I mentioned that it was opening day of the baseball season.

"You might have missed it," I said. "It actually began at 6:00 AM this morning. Sox versus the As. Sox won it in the tenth. Opening Day, and they played it in Japan. Funny how nobody thinks of starting the European soccer league in Des Moines."

I was mid-babble when I noticed that my buddy was looking right through me, as if I had said three straight sentences without any vowels. He hadn't a clue what I was talking about.

"Don't follow baseball?" I asked.

"No," he answered, "and I don't follow the
geological plates in my neighborhood."

For some reason that I have never been abl
there are people out there who find baseball bc
my own flesh and blood. My daughter, after sittin,   ᴗ
innings of the minor league Fort Wayne Wizards back in Indiana,
literally begged that I never take her to a ball game again. "Dad,"
she said, "I always thought that dying of boredom was just an
expression—until about the sixth inning of that game."

Trying to explain why I love baseball is like trying to explain to
my mother when I was nine why I tore up my good school pants
sliding into a chalk second base on a gravel playground. "But I
was safe," I whined, as if this summed up every possible reason
necessary, as well as the meaning of the sun, the moon, the stars
and all creation.

People bring up the horror stories about season-ending
strikes, steroids, human growth hormones, snot-nosed
million-dollar players and snot-nosed multimillion-dollar
owners and ask why anyone would follow the game. I respond
that baseball is baseball. It is a quintessentially Catholic sport:
the rubrics of the game, so simple yet intricate, creating its own
liturgy; the timelessness, hinting of the possibility that each
game could theoretically last for eternity; the appeal to all the
senses, from the taste of a hot dog to the smell of the outfield
grass; the ongoing murmur of a continuing, communal conversation in the stands—nothing like it in any other sport—that
accompanies every play and every pitch.

But most of all there is the hagiography. Baseball comes with
its own *Lives of the Saints,* and the true fan lives in a world where
the past and present mix in the pantheon of those who played

the game—either in yesterday's extra-inning thriller or when Calvin Coolidge was president.

The Bambino

Babe Ruth was dying. The cancer that had attacked him at a young fifty-three was eating him alive. As described in Leigh Montville's *The Big Bam*:

> A statue of Blessed Martin DePorres ...stood on the Babe's nightstand. On July 21 [1948], Ruth's condition worsened, and Father Kaufman gave him the Last Rites of the Church. It was a strangely controversial move. The priest received a lot of positive mail, but also some hate mail from Catholics who thought that Ruth's profligate life didn't deserve forgiveness. One was written entirely in ecclesiastical Latin.[1]

The greatest ballplayer who ever lived was Catholic, and for years the Knights of Columbus considered him their most valuable player. As just about the whole world knows, Ruth was raised in a Catholic orphanage, St. Mary's Industrial School in Baltimore, and he often credited his love for the game—and his unique power stroke—to Xaverian Brother Matthias Boutlier. Brother Matthias would not only offer guidance but hit towering fly balls to five hundred assembled boys who would scramble for the souvenirs, a young George Herman Ruth among them.

The Babe stayed close to St. Mary's and always spoke well of his upbringing there. In 1926 he bought Brother Matthias a new Cadillac, and he would show up at the school for fundraisers. When his Yankee coach, Miller Huggins, worried about Ruth's nightlife that same year, he paid to have Brother Matthias come to Chicago, dine with the Babe and make certain he was back in his hotel room at a reasonable hour.

Ruth identified himself with the Church, even if his life did not always mirror the faith lived well. "He would amaze teammates," Montville states, "when he would appear at Mass in the morning after a night of indulgence."[2] But the Babe once wrote—or had ghostwritten for him—"I knew an old priest once.... How I envy him. He was not trying to please a crowd. He was merely trying to please his own immortal soul.... So fame never came to him. I am listed as a famous home-runner, yet beside that obscure priest, who was so good and so wise, I never got to first base."[3]

When Babe Ruth joined the Red Sox as a rookie, he found that the Catholics on the squad had to face some old-fashioned nativism. A contingent on the team, led by future Hall of Famer Tris Speaker, adhered to that "old time religion." Anti-Catholic comments were not uncommon. Ruth, about as loud as one could get and lacking just about every social grace, became the voice of the Catholics, a defender of the faith.

It should be noted that Ruth's apologetics did not involve subtle theological debate. Mostly he relied on Rabelaisian invective and threats of violence. Fortitude can be lived in many ways.

The Babe's style might not be the best model, but you've got to admire his fortitude. We certainly spread the faith by the example of our lives, but there are times when fortitude is not a matter of manly reticence. Fortitude means a willingness to speak out for the faith, especially in public—and when it's not altogether comfortable to do so.

Brave Hearts

> "Come on, shake off the covers of this sloth,"
> the master said, "for sitting softly cushioned,
> or tucked in bed, is no way to win fame;
>
> and he whose life passes without renown,
> will leave no trace of what he was on earth
> as smoke in wind and foam upon the water."[4]

Thus Virgil advises the Pilgrim in the *Inferno* when he stops to catch his breath after an arduous climb. The Pilgrim climbs to his feet and responds, "Move on, for I am strong and ready."[5]

Fortitude is courage and constancy, the only two values we can learn from the movies. It borders on obstinacy, a willingness to hold steadfast to our principles when life is telling us not to bother. Fortitude lives in the stories we like to tell around the fire.

A buddy invited me to a women's basketball game at a local Catholic college, St. Francis University in Fort Wayne. He was an assistant coach, and he wanted me to get a look at a team that was doing pretty well. I have never been much for watching basketball—particularly the girls' game, if the truth be told. But I went along to make a friend happy.

There wasn't a bad crowd at the game, considering it was an evening in midweek and Indiana January outside. The play was fast and physical. Elbows were flying, and the pace was run-and-gun. It wasn't your mother's women's basketball.

There was a girl on my friend's team named Emily, a Catholic kid from a Catholic family. The daughter of the coach, she was a short kid who played point guard tenaciously. Emily was college-girl pretty, the kind of pretty that makes old men smile.

During the off-season Emily had been diagnosed with cancer. She had been getting the full treatment right into the season but continued somehow to play ball. The night I was there, she came into the game early.

It's funny how little things catch your eye. I noticed at one point that someone had left a brown towel just out-of-bounds underneath one of the baskets. I was surprised that nobody had scooped it up. But as I looked at it more closely, I realized it was a woman's wig.

Emily was still on the court. I don't know if she lost her wig getting knocked around under the boards or just tossed it off because it bothered her. But she was in the thick of things, still running up and down the court, playing with everything she had. Her hair, of course, was virtually gone. It had that scraggly look that anyone knows who has experienced cancer treatment. A few strands hung down limply, and it was hard to tell if these were leftover remnants or hair struggling to come back. It was matted to her naked scalp from the sweat of playing.

I know that for many cancer victims—male or female, young or old—the loss of hair is terribly crushing, and they do what they can to cover it up, particularly in public. Not too many would gainsay them the right to do so. And there was Emily, a young girl in front of a college crowd, working it.

She played the rest of the game hard. I don't know what happened to the wig. But she never put it back on.

We identify fortitude with bravery, and that's not a bad analogy. There is a bravery that we naturally admire, even if it borders on the foolish. It's not the foolish bravery of Jeff Foxworthy's most common "redneck" last words, "Hey, y'all, watch this!" It's the bravery of a guy trudging off to work every day at a job that's tearing his guts out, because his family has to eat. It's the bravery of a guy spending his leisure time trying to fight the scourge of pornography in a culture that has made the sale of sex a multibillion-dollar business. And it's Emily just out of chemo getting her wig knocked off at a small school basketball game and not giving it a thought.

There are heroes out there every day, living in the grace of fortitude. We used to call it white martyrdom, and their names were legion in the twentieth century. They were the quiet heroes who refused to abandon the faith when the knock came at the door late at night.

Born in 1891, James E. Walsh was the second of nine children. A timekeeper in a steel mill by trade, he decided on a different vocation when he heard of a new American missionary order. In 1915 he became the second priest ordained for Maryknoll. In 1918 he was one of four men sent on the first foreign mission, assigned to China. In 1927, at age thirty-six, he was ordained a bishop for China.

He stayed in China until 1936, when he returned to Maryknoll to head the order. But in 1948, at the request of the Vatican, he returned to China as head of the Catholic Central Bureau, coordinating all mission activities in the country.

For an old timekeeper, the timing was not very good. In 1949 the Chinese Communists came to power, and they immediately went after the Catholic clergy. In 1951 Father Walsh's bureau was ordered closed, and his superiors in Maryknoll worried about his safety. His response: "To put up with a little inconvenience at my age is nothing. Besides, I am a little sick and tired of being pushed around on account of my religion."[6]

But it eventually became more than just being pushed around.

He was arrested in 1959 and sentenced to twenty years in prison. After serving twelve years in isolation, he was suddenly released. Wearing a faded checkered shirt and khaki pants, a man of fortitude walked across a bridge in Hong Kong to freedom. He would die in 1981.

The *Catechism of the Catholic Church* quotes the Curé of Ars: "The priest continues the work of redemption on earth.... If we really understood the priest on earth, we would die not of fright but of love.... The Priesthood is the love of the heart of Jesus" (*CCC*, 1589, citing B. Nodet, *Jean-Marie Vianney, Curé d'Ars*, p. 100).

A Little Scripture

The action takes place in Capernaum, a town in northern Israel on the Jordan River. John the Evangelist describes it in nearly fifty verses in the sixth chapter of his Gospel. He has just told of the miracle of the loaves and fishes, by which Jesus fed five thousand men (and uncounted women and children) with only five loaves and two dried fish. When it appeared that the people would try to make him king after such a miracle, Jesus took off for the hills.

Later that evening he talked to his assembled followers about the bread from heaven—manna—that God had provided to their ancestors in the desert. He then told them that he is the "bread of life" that came down from heaven. "For this is the will of my Father, that every one who sees the Son and believes in him should have eternal life; and I will raise him up at the last day" (John 6:40).

The disciples were not amused. Some pointed out that this was Jesus, the son of Joseph. They knew his father and mother.

Where was he going with this claim that he came down from heaven, the Son of the Father? This was getting to be a bit much.

Jesus told them to quit nattering and listen. He explained it again: "I am the bread of life. Your fathers ate manna in the wilderness, and they died. This is the bread which comes down from heaven, that a man may eat of it and not die. I am the living bread which came down from heaven; if any one eats of this bread, he will live for ever; and the bread which I shall give for the life of the world is my flesh" (John 6:48–51).

That didn't work either. "What's he talking about?" they asked. "How is he going to give us his flesh to eat?" They expected Jesus to back up, explain the analogy, dissect the metaphor, have someone smart explain that what he really meant to say wasn't what he was saying.

Honest reaction—we do that ourselves with a lot of the Gospels. A priest once told me that a lot of people spend their lives hoping that Jesus didn't mean exactly what he said. Fortitude is living as if he did.

Jesus didn't back off. "As the living Father sent me, and I live because of the Father, so he who eats me will live because of me. This is the bread which came down from heaven, not such as the fathers ate and died; he who eats this bread will live for ever" (John 6:57–58).

A lot of his followers looked at Jesus, saw he wasn't metaphorically spinning a yarn and decided this was someone they need not take very seriously any longer. Jesus asked them if this shook their faith. They answered with their feet. As John describes it, many of his disciples broke away and would not remain in his company any longer (see John 6:66).

In its own way, it is comforting to know this happened to

Jesus. If he couldn't be understood, what right do we have to be understood? We spend half our lives trying to convince people of things, when Jesus himself couldn't convince his disciples of this elemental revelation. The lesson? As Saint Francis of Assisi prayed, "Grant that I may not so much seek...to be understood as to understand."[7]

But then something very interesting happened. As the disciples became former disciples, Jesus turned to the twelve—his handpicked apostles—and asked them if they wanted to take off as well. Peter answered for them: "Lord, to whom shall we go? You have the words of eternal life" (John 6:68).

And there we have it. Saint Peter is our example. Fortitude is believing and acting on our beliefs when it is hard to do so. Principles, truth, courage—they are easy virtues in easy times. It's at the shank of the evening, when belief is hard, that fortitude becomes a virtue to live by.

Monkey Business

I have never thought much of monkey humor. Even as a kid, when a monkey would make an appearance on the *Abbott and Costello Show* and the old laugh track would go off the charts, I couldn't manage a chuckle. Monkeys in bow ties, playing cards and drinking bottles of beer didn't do a thing for me.

A newspaper story a few years back claimed that social scientists studying orangutans in Borneo and elsewhere concluded that the beasties live in a social culture of their own. The observers discovered that the orangutans like to ride falling trees to the ground and jump off to safety at the last instant, show that they are displeased by making a kissing sound with a leaf pressed over their pursed lips and arrange their living quarters in patterns that serve no purpose. They also spend most of their waking hours either looking for food or eating. In other words, theirs is a culture not dissimilar to how I lived as a college sophomore.

The collective study concluded that only three species on earth have exhibited what the scientists define as culture: orangutans, chimpanzees and, you will be happy to know, humans. The scientists defined culture as the ability to learn and pass on behaviors from role models in one's immediate community. In other words, culture is learned behavior caused by our living with other humans rather than by the necessities of our physical makeup and surroundings. I play baseball, therefore I am.

I think part of the problem is that scientists sell the idea of culture much too short when they try to break it down to a simplistic definition. Imitative behavior—no matter how it is acquired—is simply monkey see, monkey do. And one of the difficulties within contemporary culture is just that: the reducing of the joy and beauty of culture to a meaningless pattern of behavior that makes the individual human being insignificant. It is the source of the mindless dictatorships of the twentieth century, sacrificing the uniqueness of an individual life to something allegedly greater: the masses, the nation or the race. It leads to ugly, dangerous and ultimately tragic thinking. But even in the best of political structures, the cultural soul of a society can be lost when the uniqueness and sacredness of the individual is lost or is sacrificed to any other perceived greater good.

The Church has a core understanding of culture. It is based not on a collective, not on imitative patterns, not on conditioned learning. The Church teaches that life is not absurd.

Every life has meaning and purpose, because every life is the creation of God, who wants us to live fully and know the truths of our existence. That is the heart of human culture. It is far more than a simple matter of searching for fun, food and finances—even among college sophomores.

Fortitude is our recognition that we must live the essential Christian understanding and do what we can to make it happen in our world. We are not created by culture: We create culture. And the world we live in is our responsibility.

The End of the World

Her name was Skeeter Davis, and she was a popular country singer in her day. Born in Appalachia as Mary Frances Penick, she was raised in poverty. Her voice led to a singing career that put her on the *Grand Ole Opry* radio show for more than forty years. That career hit its high point in 1963 with the million-selling recording of "The End of the World."

That's where I come in.

In the late spring of 1963, I was at Christ the King School in Yonkers, New York, ticking off the last days of grammar school, which at the time seemed to prove to us eighth-graders that eternity actually could come to an end. We had started together at Christ the King as wide-eyed five- and six-year-olds; we were now thirteen and fourteen, coolly confident and ready for the heady days of high school just around the corner.

A rite of passage that eighth-grade spring was the first girl-boy party, carefully monitored by parents and dreaded by most of the guys in my class. We actually dressed up in ties and jackets, while the girls wore frilly dresses and did things with their hair that we had never seen before. We stared at each other across the expanse of a classmate's backyard lit by flimsy paper lanterns in the June evening. Gorged on chips, pretzels and soda pop, everybody wondered who would make the first move.

Then Skeeter Davis was on the record player, singing her slow song about lost love and "The End of the World." Somebody asked somebody to dance, and the ice was broken.

In a dead sweat and nearly stammering, I asked Marilyn Crystal. I had secretly admired her for months, though she was six or seven inches taller than me. She knew we would look silly, but she said yes anyway. God bless her.

For all the decades since, whenever Skeeter Davis would come on an oldies radio station, I'd go back to an eighth-grade party where I first asked a girl to dance. And I'd smile, no matter what kind of day I was having.

Skeeter never hit the heights again, though she toured with Elvis Presley and, of all people, the Rolling Stones. Married three times, she also got in trouble with the *Grand Ole Opry* when she complained about the arrest in Nashville of some "Jesus Freaks" protesting against Christmas materialism. But she was still singing gospel music after age seventy, which is not bad. Then the cancer got her, and she was gone at seventy-two.

One of the mysteries of life rarely answered this side of heaven is how many we touch in the years given to us. Most of us go through our days without doing much of anything that gains celebrity status. The idea that something we might do could touch an awful lot of people seems silly. But we never know.

That old saw about a tropical storm having its genesis in the flap of a butterfly's wings in Africa can be applied for good as well. The goodness we can create in the small moments of our lives can reach far beyond us in ways that we never know—and fortitude is living our lives each day in that knowledge.

When Skeeter Davis sold a million copies of a record, she knew that people heard her sing and liked it. But she might never have realized that one song can make a difference to people, if only just for peaceful nostalgia on a tough day. And that's not a bad gift.

He Knows What He Is About

I have never been good at spontaneous prayer, except for the usual "Why me?" "Can't it wait?" and my all-time favorite, "Help!" Instead I have relied on the kindness of strangers when it comes to prayers. I find that reading the prayers of the giants of the faith does a lot more for me than any drivel I could come up with on my own.

For example, I am fond of Cardinal John Newman as a source for prayer. The nineteenth-century English convert had a rather condescending attitude toward the Irish—no matter that he was rightly frustrated in their dismissive attitude toward him—but I have forgiven him for that, generous soul that I am.

Here is one of my favorite prayers from Newman:

> God has created me to do Him some definite service. He has committed some work to me which He has not committed to another. I have my mission. I may never know it in this life, but I shall be told it in the next. I am a link in a chain, a bond of connection between persons. He has not created me for naught. I shall do good; I shall do His work. I shall be an angel of peace, a preacher of truth in my own place, while not intending it if I do but keep His commandments. Therefore, I will trust Him, whatever I am, I can never be thrown away. If I am in sickness, my sickness

> may serve Him, in perplexity, my perplexity may serve
> Him. If I am in sorrow, my sorrow may serve Him. He does
> nothing in vain. He knows what He is about. He may take
> away my friends. He may throw me among strangers. He
> may make me feel desolate, make my spirits sink, hide my
> future from me. Still, He knows what He is about.[8]

Great stuff. But here's an interesting twist.

I was wandering around the Internet looking up some Newman for a little research. I stumbled onto a Catholic site where the above prayer was reproduced. I took a moment to read it, needing a little spiritual tea and sympathy on a workday afternoon. But something struck me as wrong.

The prayer seemed "nice" but not as moving and self-effacing (as all good prayer should be) as my memory of it. Then I realized that someone had done a little bowdlerizing to Newman. They had omitted the line "I shall be an angel of peace, a preacher of truth in my own place, while not intending it if I do but keep His commandments." It was a curious omission because, at least in my reading, it altered the meaning of the prayer completely.

Newman's point was not that he was "a chain," "an angel of peace" and "a preacher of truth in my own place" because of any inherent personal greatness in him. Newman was saying that he could become these things, even if he didn't consciously intend to be these things, if he kept the commandments. If he lived the way of Christian life in complete trust in the Lord, his "mission" would be accomplished, even though he might never know what that mission was. Because the Lord knows "what He is about."

That summarizes fortitude for every guy. We live it by living the commandments, by loving God and loving neighbor. Fortitude gives our lives purpose in and of itself. Fortitude is the belief that God did not create us in vain. He gave us a purpose, even if we don't always see it clearly. Fortitude is trust lived—because God knows "what He is about."

The Babe Exits

Every Catholic family should have a baseball story—a story to tell when the sun breaks a bit more warmly in early April, and every fan shares a new beginning with the world itself. My Catholic family had a baseball story when I was growing up.

It wasn't the story of my brother's being nearly run over by Phil Rizzuto, the Hall of Fame Yankee shortstop from the 1950s. My brother was standing on the sidewalk outside Yankee Stadium on game day. Though he was perfectly in the right and minding his own business, a cop yelled at him to "move it!" when Rizzuto was backing his ocean liner of a car over the curb, nearly hitting my brother. The cop then gave Rizzuto—no longer a Yankee shortstop but a Yankee announcer—a smiling welcome. The lesson clearly taught at a young age: "Them that has, got it; them that don't, don't."

Our real Catholic family baseball story involved the greatest of them all, George Herman Ruth. After the Babe died on August 16, 1948, his body lay in state at the entrance to Yankee Stadium for two days, allowing a crowd of a hundred thousand to pay their respects. The funeral Mass was then held at St. Patrick's Cathedral, and Ruth was buried at Gate of Heaven Cemetery in Hawthorne, New York.

Two of those hundred thousand who went by the Babe's casket at Yankee Stadium were my Old Man and my oldest brother. The

Old Man was a still a young man then, a strapping, blond-haired thirty-year-old guy. My brother was just a small fry. I wasn't even a rumor yet.

As they went by the casket, the Old Man scooped up my brother so he could get a better look. He held him over the Babe for a few seconds, then they moved on. My brother recalls to this day that all he saw was a shrunken old guy who was obviously dead. My brother is not a romantic—or much of a baseball fan.

But here's the catch: Nearly every time the newsreel of that day is shown, it includes footage of the Old Man holding my brother over the Babe's casket. Now, you can only see them from the top and behind, because of the way they would place the cameras in those days. So we could never be absolutely certain that it was actually them in the newsreel. But the Old Man was certain.

And that's our Catholic family baseball story.

For Emily
Emily is cancer free. She doesn't play basketball anymore—young women almost never seem to play once they graduate—but she works out regularly with tennis and volleyball. When I got in touch with her years after that night on the basketball court, she had just married a former football player from Poland. She is a lawyer now, with a specialty in domestic work and adoptions.

"Sometimes life gets moving so fast that it is easy to lose track of the memories of the time I was sick," she told me. "Every now and again it feels good to remember how far I've come since then."

Fortitude is a virtue especially appropriate to the bad times. And when it is really part of us, we can even forget we have it.

CHAPTER THREE

{Temperance}

Temperance is the virtue of keeping our desires and wishes within honorable limits. It is moderation in all things, so that we rule our passions and are not ruled by them. It is learning to appreciate the role of all of God's creation in our lives, without abusing the gifts he has given. Temperance is the virtue of a balanced life.

I was sitting at the ballpark with a buddy, watching the Pittsburgh Pirates and the San Diego Padres perform woefully. Anybody can watch a good baseball game; it's only the true fan who can suffer through a bad one.

Like everybody at every ballpark, we were talking baseball old and new. Examining the Pirates' chances to hit the five-hundred mark by season's end, recalling a catch made on some ancient field in the old hometown and comparing the ball players of our youth, forever frozen in the mind's eye from a point in time decades past.

In a lull in the conversation, my buddy asked, "So how are the twins doing?"

I responded, "What do I care about the Twins? I'm a Mets fan."
A moment's pause. "I mean your twin grandkids."
Another moment's pause. "Oh. They're OK."

Sometimes our priorities can get a little out of whack. That's where temperance comes in.

The Blessing of Beer
Benedictio Cerevisiae, from the old Roman Ritual, is an ancient blessing of the Church:

> **V.** Our help is in the name of the Lord.
> **R.** Who made heaven and earth.
> **V.** The Lord be with you.
> **R.** And with thy spirit.
> Let us pray.
> Bless, + O Lord, this creature beer, which thou hast deigned to produce from the fat of grain, that it may be a salutary remedy to the human race; and grant, through the invocation of thy holy name, that whoever shall drink it may gain health in body and peace in soul. Through Christ our Lord.
> **R.** Amen.

One of God's tender mercies is a cold beer on a warm night with a good friend—"a salutary remedy to the human race." There are those good souls among us who need to substitute lemonade—they have the Problem, as my Irish American mother called it—but the pleasure is all the same. And they are smart enough to know that.

Temperance is a virtue that gives men pause. We identify temperance with the teetotaler who avoids a beer out of prissiness rather than addiction. Unlike prudence, fortitude and justice, which we all admire even when we struggle to live up to them, temperance seems to be the opposite of passion, that driving force that pushes us to excel. Temperance becomes a celebration of the wishy-washy, an unmanly substitution of the charbroiled steak of life with a limp salad of existence. It baptizes the ordinary at the expense of the exceptional. Temperance is the Pirates at five hundred.

But even in the practical scheme of things, that's not temperance. Temperance is having that beer because we want it to enjoy, not because we need it to enjoy. Temperance is taking a big slice of that steak while not forgetting that the great life will always have a salad that goes with it. Temperance is knowing that if most of the hours in a day are made up of living the ordinary well, the exceptional will take care of itself. Temperance is hoping the Pirates will do better but knowing that nothing beats fun at the old ballpark, as the Cub announcer Harry Caray told us, win or lose. Temperance is knowing how to live passionately without living by our passions.

Men fail temperance when they fail perspective, when they forget John Lennon's immortal advice that life is what happens while we are busy making other plans. Our temperance fails when we start substituting: when money, sex and power (or looks, strength, booze, pills, sports, success—I could go on and on) take over as the controlling elements in our lives. Temperance fails when we define ourselves by things we are not—like a job—and see other people as either stumbling blocks or useful means to whatever we want. Temperance fails when perspective vanishes and we begin to see the ephemeral as the eternal.

Alcoholics Anonymous meetings always begin and end with the Serenity Prayer, attributed to Reinhold Niebuhr:

> God, grant me the serenity
> to accept the things I cannot change;
> courage to change the things I can;
> and wisdom to know the difference.
>
> Living one day at a time;
> enjoying one moment at a time;
> accepting hardships as the path to peace;
>
> Taking, as He did, this sinful world
> as it is, not as I would have it;
> trusting that He will make all things right
> if I surrender to His will;
> that I may be reasonably happy in this life
> and supremely happy with Him
> forever in the next.
> Amen.

Temperance is serenity that comes with wisdom. It is the hope for reasonable and faith-filled happiness in this life, with the expectation of supreme happiness in the next.

What a Wonderful World

One day was falling into the next, and the misery index on the job was climbing. Long days. Long worries. Long face. My head was about to explode after living at my desk, lo, these past few weeks, so I took off a little toward the shank of a summer's day. I craved two things: not a word and not a thought. The plan was to change the brain to eggplant through television reruns.

My son was home from college, and the second I slithered through the door, he was on me. "We're going flying," he said. He had taken up flying model airplanes that he built himself. I was impressed with his enthusiasm, but the hobby left me cold.

He inherited his skill at building stuff from my father-in-law. I could barely build a healthy argument, let alone a replica of a World War II fighter.

"I don't think so," I said.

But he took the briefcase from my hand, set it by the television and told me that he thought *The Simpsons* and *Seinfeld* could do without me. "We're out of here. Grab that toolbox."

The "airport" was a mowed field out in the country with a little chicken wire to mark it off from a dirt parking lot. There was one other truck there, nicely appointed with just the right touch of rust, and a slightly rusted old geezer to go with it. He had a mound of stuff on a paint-peeled picnic table, and he was tinkering away on his own plane. Which is why I don't have hobbies—I don't have the patience for tinkering, and hobbies are all about tinkering.

My son lugged all his stuff over by the old geezer, and they commenced to speak all things model aircraft. I hung at the fringes, not knowing a gasket from a flange, while they chatted on. Every once in a while they'd toss me a bone—"Beautiful day, huh?"—and I'd smile and mumble something banal in return. It was OK.

As there was absolutely nothing I could contribute, the brain was catching up on its beauty sleep. I had time to look up at a sky so blue and clear that I had to shade my eyes even though the sun was heading toward the horizon. The field outside the landing strip was filled with unmowed hay, Queen Anne's lace and wild daisies and daffodils with their buds turned white, ready to blow away on the first breeze.

"She loves me; she loves me not," I thought, going back to sixth-grade crushes.

"I think I'm ready to get it started," my son told the old geezer directly and me indirectly, after unknown time had passed widgeting widgets.

"It's ready to get started," the old geezer confirmed, and I nodded agreeably, as I most often do when I don't have a clue. Woody Allen said that 90 percent of success is just showing up. The other 10 percent is an agreeable nod done in ignorance.

I helped my son take the model plane out to the field, where he positioned it for takeoff. With the control box he began to rev the engine, which impressed me to no end. I was assuming none of this would ever work, like the guy with his hands in his pockets when the Wright Brothers were setting up at Kitty Hawk.

He took it down the runway, gave it a little extra goose, and up it went. I was suitably gob-smacked, as excited as a little kid when a firecracker goes off. Dips and curls, runway touches and takeoffs, cruising off over distant hills, attempting a lower-level dive at my head. It was a wonder to see, and I took pure joy in the plane and in my son's pure joy.

One fancy maneuver too many, and the plane took a tumble into a low-lying cornfield. We dug it out, and it looked a wreck to me.

"Fixing it is as much fun as flying it—well, almost," my son told me, while the old geezer advised that crashes are the reason he always brings two planes. My son didn't have the fixings to fix it, so we packed it back into the truck. The old geezer and my son swapped model airplane war stories for a few more minutes, then it was time to go. I realized that we had killed more than two summer evening hours and that we were both getting hungry.

There was a tavern in a small town nearby, where the burgers were thick and greasy, the fries so crisp that they sounded like raw carrots when you snapped them. He had a beer, I had a root beer, and the food went down fine.

We talked of flying, college, football, his fishing expeditions when he was a kid, the house I grew up in. We talked of old dogs and new cars, golf lies and baseball truths, his sister's gymnastics and his mother's heroics, which reminded me finally that we'd better get home.

Outside the moon was blue, and the summer sky was filled with stars. We craned our necks and didn't say a word.

As we carried the wreckage of his model airplane into the house, my daughter laughed, and my wife's eyes rolled in mock horror at the carnage. I sat down, smiled and spotted my briefcase where I had left it. I decided that I was ready to take it to work the next morning.

And I could hear Louis Armstrong singing about "skies of blue and clouds of white." And I had to think, "Yes, what a wonderful world."

A Little Scripture

Dante, always with a kind thought, talks about temperance in his own way:

> Your earthly fame is but a gust of wind
> that blows about, shifting this way and that,
> and as it changes quarter, changes name.
>
> Were you to reach the ripe old age of death,
> instead of dying prattling in your crib,
> would you have more fame in a thousand years?[1]

Dante asks us to consider the fleeting things we latch on to as if they will make all the difference in the world. Fame? Well, most of us are forgotten before we're gone, let alone a thousand years from now. Lead the great life in faith, and set your eyes on more than the baubles and gewgaws the world hands out, he is telling us. All the trinkets will disappear anyway, and many of the things we determinedly pursue are not what makes us who we are or what we want to be for the long haul.

Luke tells us that the little guy—his name was Zacchaeus—couldn't see over the crowds. Zacchaeus was a tax collector, and like most tax collectors at any age of any time, he was a wealthy man. And not too well liked on both accounts.

Jesus had come to Jericho, and Zacchaeus wanted to catch a look at the man everyone was talking about. So with the crowds blocking his line of vision, he ran ahead and scurried up a tree.

But then something happened. Arriving at the tree, Jesus stopped, looked up and spotted our tax collector. "Zacchaeus," he shouted up to him, "come down quickly. For today I must stay at your house."

And Zacchaeus scampered back down the tree, no doubt the happiest guy in the neighborhood. He had been called. He had been chosen. Not bad for a wealthy tax collector.

As always seems to happen in the Gospel accounts, somebody was not happy with Jesus going to stay at the house of Zacchaeus. "He's a sinner," they grumbled, a rotten tax collector who had made himself a lot of money in the process.

Jesus probably cracked a brief smile and turned to Zacchaeus, as if to ask, "What do you have to say for yourself?" This happens a lot to short guys. They always have to explain.

"Well," Zacchaeus said, "I'll give half of everything I've got to the poor. And if I have cheated anybody, I'll pay them back four times over." And Jesus said, "Today salvation has come to this house" (see Luke 19:1 - 9).

It's not the job; it's what we do with the job. Temperance teaches us that we are not what we do but who we are. Then we can have a good answer when Jesus shows up to announce that today he's coming to our house.

There's always that search for balance, which is what temperance is all about. On the one hand Jesus reminds us:

> Therefore I tell you, do not be anxious about your life, what you shall eat or what you shall drink, or about your body, what you shall put on. Is not life more than food and the body more than clothing? Look at the birds of the air: they neither sow nor reap nor gather into barns, and yet your heavenly Father feeds them. Are you not of more value than they? And which of you by being anxious can add one cubit to his span of life? And why are you anxious about clothing? Consider the lilies of the field, how they grow; they neither toil nor spin; yet I tell you, even Solomon in all his glory was not clothed like one of these. (Matthew 6:25– 29)

But right after his encounter with Zacchaeus, Jesus told the parable of the ten pounds (see Luke 19:11–27). A nobleman about to embark on a journey gave ten of his servants some money and told them to do what they could with it. Upon his return, one servant came forward and reported that his pound had been wisely invested and earned the nobleman more money. A second reported that his investment had also reaped a profit. A third said that he had been frightened of losing his coin, so he had buried it. The nobleman cursed this last man for doing nothing. The last thing the Lord expects of us is to take the talents—the coins he gives to each of us—and fail to do anything with them.

So temperance does imply a certain balancing act. On the one hand, temperance is our way of acknowledging that we are far more than the sum of our careers. Yet temperance teaches as well that our talents are given to us so that they—not we—might flourish in our hands.

God's Work

It was a hot day, and I was putting down some mulch around the outside of the house. It is one of those chores that the spouse tells you to do, you do it, and you don't have a clue why you are doing it.

It was getting late in the afternoon, and I was covered with the stuff. I took a brief break, leaning against a tree, and stared down at my hands. They looked as if I had been in a prizefight.

It's funny how little things stick with you from when you were a kid. Wisps of memory come without bidding, short stories that should have been forgotten long ago.

The old monsignor who was our pastor at Christ the King Parish in Yonkers would routinely drop by our fourth-grade class to give a little message. One of his favorite chats was to remind us that *good-bye* was a secular contraction of "God be with you." He thought it the mark of a good Catholic to part company with the traditional expression. When he took his leave, we would stand and chant in unison, "God be with you, Monsignor!" He had it inscribed on our school pencils.

One day the monsignor showed up at the door with a man in

tow. The gentleman was a bit disheveled-looking, wearing old brown work pants and dusty shoes. He also wore a sheepish smile, a little bit embarrassed by what was to come next.

"Children," the monsignor announced, "this man is here to work on your church. He is cleaning the statues, oiling the pews, polishing the floors. Now, I want you to look at these hands."

And he had the man show us his hands, palms up, as if we were checking to see whether he had washed before lunch.

"These calloused hands," the Monsignor said, "do God's work." Then they turned to leave.

"God be with you, Monsignor and Mister!"

One time I visited a Catholic high school on Long Island— Bishop Kellenberg Memorial High School. It is run by the Marianist community of priests and brothers, a legendary teaching order founded in France. The school also serves as the provincial residence of the order.

The priest-principal was proudly showing off the new chapel that was under construction for the priests and brothers. It was on the third floor of the high school. He pointed to this and that, describing the work that was going on as we moved among saw-horses, drop cloths and half-empty work buckets. A local asked, "Who is the contractor handling this for you, Father?"

The priest smiled. "Well, we do most of the work ourselves." He went on to describe the thousands of pieces of tiled inlay that the priests and brothers had crafted to place above the altar and what it took to tear down and rebuild the walls. "You must understand," the priest explained to us, "we can't be only philosophers and theologians. We need to be plumbers and car-penters as well."

As the good monsignor told us in fourth grade, it's God's work.

Snow Day

One image could sum up the difference between how kids are raised now and how kids were raised then: monkey bars. When I was a kid, monkey bars were all the rage in playgrounds and schoolyards. They were metal contraptions that kids could climb all over like, well, monkeys. The thing that added that little zest was that there was a good chance you could fall off while trying to reach out to "tag" a buddy as you played.

To catch you when you fell, concerned administrators, parents and other caregivers had monkey bars fixed in a solid base of concrete. This would assure an abrupt but certain landing and maybe a broken bone or two. You learned that, no matter the fun, life had its hard lessons. Literally.

The monkey bars theory of child-rearing extended to other moments. My mother, for example, did not believe in "snow days." Since we all walked to school, she would pack us off no matter the wintry catastrophes lurking outside the hearth. We were pretty well convinced that if the Russians lobbed a couple of ICBMs at downtown Yonkers, my mother would simply offer a stern admonition not to lollygag on the way to school.

One time Yonkers got smacked with an overnight ice storm. We about had to crawl our way to school. When we got there only about twenty kids scattered over eight grades had managed to make it in. It being the way things were done then, the nuns sent us crawling back home, warning us not to lollygag.

We didn't complain. We got a day off. And as everybody knows, there is nothing better than a snow day when you are a kid in grammar school. It was as if the fates had dropped a shining ball in the midst of the dreary eternity that was Monday through Friday.

I had my own snow day recently. A stiff one had blown in from the south and west one Tuesday in February. I listened not once but twice to the recorded phone message telling me that work was shut down.

I hadn't had a snow day in years. My wife seemed uninterested in my suggestions of a sleigh ride or a snowball fight, though they were the only things I really had been trained to do with a snow day. So I watched the weather channel, cooked the wife some breakfast, caught part of an old Cary Grant movie on television before realizing I had actually seen it when it was first released, picked up a book on the French and Indian War that I had been meaning to start, let the dog out, let the dog back in, then wondered if I should take a nap—at 10:13 in the morning.

Finally I figured out what to do. Use the time wisely, and catch up on some stuff from work that needed to get done. One of the marvels of the computer age is that we're just a click away from work.

In his tender mercy the good Lord had given me a snow day, and I didn't know what to do with it. So I worked. I think he's going to ask me about that when the time comes.

Al McGuire, the late Marquette University basketball coach, television commentator and Catholic philosopher of the highest order, advised that every so often on the way to work, we've got to turn left instead of right. Take an unplanned day off out of nowhere to nowhere. It's advice that doesn't fit with our culturally Protestant work ethic. But as I said, Coach Al was a Catholic philosopher.

Our goal is to find our vocation and live it. That's why the Church speaks so highly of the inherent dignity of work. Our vocation—our work—is a gift and a grace; it is what we do to share in God's creation. But at the same time, our work is not our life. As we are called to share in God's creation, we are also called to enjoy God's creation. The Sabbath—the day of rest—"was made for man, not man for the sabbath" (Mark 2:27). Temperance understands that.

A Giant Story

The year was 1986, and the New York Giants had just won the Super Bowl 39–20 against the Denver Broncos. Phil Simms, the Giants' quarterback, was going to Disneyland, and all was right with the world.

I had watched the game at home with a couple of buddies. The Giants won by racking up twenty-four straight unanswered points in the second half, while I guzzled down who knows how many unanswered beers. The last time the Giants had been in a championship game was 1963. I was thirteen, and I watched with my Old Man and my brothers as they lost to the Chicago Bears 14–10.

I came to football awareness just as the pro game was really taking off. One of my earliest memories of professional football was sitting in the car at a traffic light with the Old Man as two guys with an obvious snoot full strolled merrily in front of us waving football pennants. The Old Man said, "They must have been at the Giants game," and he was referring to the 1956 championship, when the Giants beat the Bears 47–7. I had just turned seven. I might not have become such a big Giants fan if I knew that my own kids would be ten years old before the team would win another championship.

But it was the halcyon days of Giants football back then. I really caught the fever when the Giants lost to the Colts in the

1958 overtime championship game, still called the greatest game ever played. They would be back in the championship game—forerunner of today's Super Bowl—in 1959, 1961, 1962 and 1963. I followed it all with a passion bordering on blind zealotry. And they lost every time.

After that loss to the Bears in 1963, true futility set in: a twenty-three-year drought from championship games that included some awful football teams. It wasn't as if the Giants were near misses during those more than two decades. There was nothing near about most of those misses. They stunk up the place.

I only attended one Giants game in person. My brother managed to get two seats in Yankee Stadium in 1971, just a few weeks before I was to leave my childhood home for a new life in Indiana. And the Giants were blown out by a vastly superior Colts team.

Did I complain during those decades about how badly the Giants played? Of course I did. But I remained their biggest fan. Living in Indiana in the days before ESPN and the Internet, I gulped down any drop of information I could get on the Giants, scanning the papers and sports magazines for news about them. I watched televised highlights of their misery faithfully. All this, year in and year out, thinking every August when preseason began that this season was going to be different. And it never was.

Until it happened. Watching the Giants dominate the Broncos in the second half, I nearly wept as a lifetime's devotion was rewarded—though it may have been the beer.

It was the day after that Super Bowl win that I had my little epiphany. Crawling out of bed, slightly hungover, a week's worth of work was ahead. I stared at myself in the mirror, trying to get up the energy to shave. I had spent about twenty-eight years imagining what life would be like after the Giants won a Super Bowl championship. And I got my answer: Life would simply go on, just as it had after every losing season. Nothing had changed. I don't know if I expected a congratulatory telegram from the Giants front office, but I do know that I began to wonder about all the time and emotional energy I had invested in them over the decades.

Now, I admit I wasn't exactly darning socks in 1990 when Scott Norwood's field goal attempt sailed wide right and the Giants won their second Super Bowl 20–19 over the Buffalo Bills, or when the Giants shocked the New England Patriots in 2008. We find grace in the stuff of this world, and there are worse things we can spend our time on than being a fan. But the Church teaches that the key is always moderation, whether in swilling beer or watching football.

Saving our passion for the things that really matter—that's temperance.

Getting in Shape

I had been working hard to get out of shape. After a burst of creative physical energy that lasted most of a decade—one final push against the years—I had settled into a comfortable inertia.

You can do about anything in this culture without fear of judgment. We're left with only a few taboos: smoking, eating red meat more than twice a month, supporting the designated hitter rule and failing to exercise regularly. In an otherwise placid sea of toleration, we are highly intolerant of these few remaining social abominations. Just as Hoosiers will never confess to still being in bed even if you call at 5:30 AM on a Saturday, Americans will sooner own up to random acts of cold-blooded murder than admit that their existence is sedentary.

So there I was, feeling guilty as only a daily overload of cultural propaganda can make one feel guilty. Like most poor souls after the last pepperoni pizza, or after a perfectly sunny afternoon spent on the couch watching the Pirates blow another one, I finally muttered, "I gotta get back in shape." (One of life's lessons in maturity is that once you have to say that, you generally will never be in shape again, no matter what you do. You can't fight city hall, and you can't fight gravity.)

Fooled by my good intentions, I wandered into the local sporting goods store, thinking of picking up a new pair of sneakers along with a set of weights to build a little muscle tone. There was a kid standing in front of a display of about eight thousand sneakers. He'd seen my kind before.

"Can I help you, sir?"

"I'm looking for a pair of sneakers."

"Sneakers?" he drawled with a mix of disgust and derision, as if I had asked him if I could use his pencil to clean out my ears. "We have all kinds of shoes, sir—tennis shoes, basketball shoes, running shoes, walking shoes, exercise shoes, baseball shoes. What specifically did you have in mind?"

"Sneakers," I said, feeling about as lost as I did in the second month of freshman algebra.

Over in the "Strength Cavalcade," events took on a similar Kafkaesque air. A fellow who looked like a brick wall struggled to get around his own muscles to shake my hand, then gave me a big "How ya doin'? My name's Ferd. What's yours?"

"Ferd," I said, "I'm Bob."

He smiled. "And what can I do for Mr. Bob?"

I really hate that kind of stuff.

"Bob's looking for a starter set of weights," I answered, "looking to get back in shape."

He sized me up and down, then announced that he had just the thing. He gathered me over to a shelf where sat a display of vinyl weights that looked like what my wife used after the kids were born. They were color coordinated—yellow, blue and, I swear, pink—and lodged on a cute little plastic shelf. The whole thing looked like a decorating tip from *Family Circle* magazine.

"Bob's weights?" I asked.

"Perfect to get you going, Bob," he answered with a pat on my back.

I might have bought them. But when Ferd took off to another more promising customer, I discovered I couldn't lift the box they came in. So it goes.

We live in a world of contrasts that make little or no sense. We are at the point where we literally make ourselves sick to stay healthy but care less and less about what the nuns called the "state of our immortal souls." If there is a forgotten virtue, it most assuredly is temperance: the virtue of living our lives in balance and moderation.

As my friend and I watched the Pirates lose to the Padres and I confused my grandchildren with an American League ball club, I realized that the saints were right: We emphasize all kinds of distractions at a danger to our immortal souls. In the end all is vanity.

At least I think that's what the saints said. In any case that's my excuse, and I'm sticking to it.

.

.

.

.

.

.

CHAPTER FOUR

{Justice}

The virtue of looking for harmony and the common good in all our actions, justice means knowing that we not only define ourselves by our basic beliefs but act in concert with them. It means that we seek the good for all of God's creation and by our lives try to create harmony and peace in our world. Justice means understanding that God has created us to live his love, and our lives will be judged accordingly. God's justice gives fundamental meaning to every life.

The funeral Mass was for the father of a friend—a business friend, which means that I knew a lot about the fellow from work but only hints of his life at home, his real life. I had never met his father, so I couldn't even put a face to the man being buried. We've all been there and wondered if we should be. Looking at a heartbroken guy I knew from office jokes, business lunches and the give-and-take of the nine-to-five world, I began to feel like a stranger at a gathering too personal for outsiders. I was observing a family in mourning whom I didn't really know; I was an interloper at a most private moment. But it's called bury-ing the dead, and our faith counts it a work of mercy.

When my mother was a girl, she and her classmates at Catholic grammar school once were summoned mid-geography class to the parish church. A transient—or what they called a "bum" back then—had died, and there was no one to claim him. The city had bought a casket and supplied the plot, while the cops called the church. And the kids in my mother's class were at the funeral Mass, even though he was a stranger to them all.

The idea was that no life should go out alone, so the kids sub-stituted for a family that didn't exist or didn't care. The kids sang "O Sacred Head Surrounded" for the guy in the cheap cas-ket. Whenever my mother heard that hymn down through the decades, she remembered a man whom no one remembered when he was alive.

That's how they taught about the work of burying the dead back then. It was a no-nonsense faith in a no-nonsense world.

My business friend's father had his funeral Mass at a small church in a small town that sits on the Allegheny River. The gas station sells pizza and fried chicken to go with a fill-up, and the locals will tell you that a couple of scenes from an old Richard Gere movie were filmed there. The jobs that were once there are not there anymore, a tale told a hundred times over in the river towns of southwestern Pennsylvania.

His father had been a union man, so the guys from the hall were there to serve as pallbearers. He was old enough to have an old man's funeral, the mourners just a few outside of family. There is always a crowd to say good-bye to old women when their time comes. If men live too long, it seems as if the mourn-ers have all gone on before them.

Big Rock Candy Mountain

Dante's *Divine Comedy* is centered on justice. All those horrific punishments detailed in his visions of hell and purgatory—the flames of hot ash, souls frozen in ice, eyes sewn shut—are Dante's imaginative punishments for those who refused to live as God intended. As the sinners had lived in *contrapasso* to justice on earth, they would exist in *contrapasso* for all eternity.

Crossing into hell, they were "cursing God, cursing their own parents, / the human race, the time, the place, the seed / of their beginning, and their day of birth."[1] They condemned all existence, because they had never acknowledged in their lives the justice at the heart of existence.

There is a folk radio station that I listen to, but only when my wife isn't in the car. The ballads from the old left bore her, but I get a kick out of them. Not because I'm a revolutionary, one of those poor souls who never got out of the sixties or curse the fates because they weren't alive in the sixties. To the contrary, though I lived through the sixties, I didn't take much of a radical turn.

But I like the music of the old left, the kind of stuff from the 1920s and 1930s that would teach Bob Dylan what he needed to know. It told the stories of helpless men shouting in the wind of life's unfairness. It was a cry for justice in a world that seemed to move at the whim of unseen forces that kept a working guy down. Not dissimilar to our own day.

When I was a kid, Burl Ives had cut a popular take on "The Big Rock Candy Mountain," a song you can still hear on music compilations for kids. Old Burl described a heavenly place for little kids, where you could hear "the buzzing of the bees on the peppermint trees 'round the soda water fountains, where the lemonade springs and the bluebird sings."

The original lyrics, played in the old train yards where men with no work gathered during the tough times, told of a slightly different utopia, an escape from a world of cops and strong-arm bosses. Cigarettes grew on trees, not peppermint leaves, "and the little streams of alcohol come a trickling down the rocks."

Imagine singing that version to a bunch of six-year-olds, though I had my dance with American social populism when I was about that age. It was at a place called Trout Lake, a family vacation paradise in the mountains of upstate New York. Trout Lake had cabins with neither hot water nor lights but a stream-fed lake that could just about ice over on an August afternoon. The Old Man loved it. Every Saturday night at Trout Lake there would be a shindig at the main house, complete with cake, punch and electric lights supplied by the owners. The guests provided the entertainment.

Somehow I was coaxed into singing at this gathering. I think it was the Old Man's doing, as he was a natural ham and enjoyed nothing more than whooping it up in front of an audience. He figured at least one of his kids would be the same way, though none of us ever satisfied that itch for him.

You would figure I'd sing a little kids' song—"The Bear Went Over the Mountain" or "The Itsy-Bitsy Spider." Nope. There I was, four feet tall and probably forty-five pounds soaking wet, standing in front of a crowd belting out Tennessee Ernie Ford's classic "Sixteen Tons."

The song told of mine workers hauling coal and never getting even with their bill at the company-owned store. It came pretty close to indentured servitude. The song's final lament is that the working man can't even afford to die. And there I was, belting out that happy tune!

But what did I know? I was just a kid, and except for a few hymns caught at Sunday Mass, old Tennessee Ernie's lyrics were the only ones I knew.

It reaches out to you, that old folk music. Not as some political and ideological agenda that wouldn't work anyway—man-made solutions to a spiritual problem are a waste of everybody's time. No, it's the voices that you hear, and it is not surprising that the old-time folk music is closely connected to old time gospel music. At the heart of it all is a perfect scriptural explanation. Like old union men, the songs tell of a "hunger and thirst for justice" (see Matthew 5:6).

A Little Scripture
Blessed Mother Teresa of Calcutta had more great stories than anybody, because great stories always come along for the ride with a life lived right. She told us through example to give unselfishly to the poor in the hardest of circumstances, because she saw Christ in each and every one of them.

One man she recalled was a foul-mouthed blasphemer who gave her sisters a terrible time. He filthied himself purposely, threw food and cursed anyone who tried to help him. After one particularly excruciating night with him, the nuns were exasperated. Mother Teresa remarked, "Well, that was Christ in his more distressing form."

John the Baptist had been arrested, and Jesus had begun his public preaching, according to the Gospel of Matthew. It was just after he had called his first apostles. He had been walking by the Sea of Galilee when he saw two brothers—Simon, whom he would name Peter, "the Rock," and Andrew. They were throwing their nets into the sea, trying to make a day's living.

"Follow me, and I will make you fishers of men" (Mark 1:17), Jesus said, in one of the puns he seemed to enjoy. He was drafting workingmen.

He saw James and his brother fishing from a boat with their father. He called to them, and they left both boat and father—which reminds me of the old Dylan line warning parents: "Don't criticize what you don't understand."

Jesus' fame was spreading because of his miraculous cures and his preaching. Crowds would follow him, waiting to see what he would do and say next. At one point he retreated to a mountain and sat down to rest. His disciples came to him, and he started to teach.

It was the Sermon on the Mount, and he began with what we call the Beatitudes. He blessed the poor in spirit, those who mourn, the humble, the merciful, the peacemakers and the pure—all those struggling to live the great life when the odds are stacked against them. He didn't promise them answers in this world, and he most assuredly promised them no great victories, no great successes in this life. But he promised them an answer for after all is said and done, when he blessed those "who hunger and thirst for righteousness, for they shall be satisfied" (Matthew 5:6).

Later, nearing the end of his public ministry, Jesus told his followers of that time when the Son of Man would return. He would divide all the people into two halves, "as a shepherd separates the sheep from the goats."

The sheep, on his right, he would tell why they were blessed and why they would enter God's eternal kingdom: "For I was hungry and you gave me food, I was thirsty and you gave me drink, in prison and you came to me." The good souls would ask when they had done this. And the Son of Man would answer: "As you did it to one of the least of these my brethren, you did it to me" (Matthew 25:31–40).

Justice doesn't always come searching for us in the way we like. Sometimes justice comes in its more distressing form.

Martyrdom, With or Without Justice

There was an auction in London a while back of a seventeenth-century book containing the trial proceedings of Father Henry Garnet, then superior of the Jesuits in England, and others allegedly involved in the famous "Gunpowder Plot" of 1605. The book contains original accounts of speeches and evidence from the trials collected by Robert Barker, printer to the king, just months after the trial of Father Garnet. The book is called *A True and Perfect Relation of the Whole Proceedings Against the Late Most Barbarous Traitors, Garnet a Jesuit and His Confederates*.

The Gunpowder Plot was the failed conspiracy to blow up Parliament and King James I in the late fall of 1605. The plot was undertaken by a small group of Catholics determined to bring an end to Protestant hegemony in England and to persecution of Catholics. The plot was discovered, and the conspirators either killed or arrested.

This is a minimalist description of a complicated historical event. Some argue to this day that the plot was cooked up by the government to make Catholics look bad. I don't buy that. I think the young Catholic conspirators were guilty as sin. But it is clear that the government used the conspiracy to wage war against the remnant Catholic community in England.

Not content with executing the conspirators, the English secretary of state, Robert Cecil, went after the underground priests. He hunted particularly the Jesuits, who were known as convincing evangelizers for Catholicism. Cecil's goal was nothing less than to use the Gunpowder Plot for a massive pogrom aimed at Catholics.

Father Garnet was caught and charged with treason. Though he and the other Jesuits in England had consistently argued against violent resistance to the penal laws inflicted on Catholics since the reign of Queen Elizabeth, Cecil was unmoved. Father Garnet was tortured and subjected to a mock trial. The outcome was never in doubt.

As he was led to the hangman on May 3, 1606, Father Garnet urged Catholics in the crowd of onlookers to pray for him. The government had hinted that there would be a dramatic last-second conversion of Father Garnet to the new orthodoxy, and someone called out, "It is expected you should recant." To which Father Garnet answered: "God forbid. I never had any such meaning, but ever meant to die a true and perfect Catholic."[2]

It was common practice for a felon convicted of treason to be hanged but kept alive so that the living body could be drawn and quartered and the still beating heart ripped out for all to see. When Father Garnet was tossed off the ladder, the crowd surged forward and pulled down on the priest's legs, killing him quickly so that he would be spared the horrific final torture.

It was said that a husk from the straw basket that caught Father Garnet's severed head was stained with the priest's blood in a way that miraculously resembled his face. The husk was placed in a reliquary, hidden at the Spanish embassy and eventually smuggled to Catholic Europe, where it was venerated for many years. It was lost in the chaos of the French Revolution.

Why was the book containing the records of the trial so valuable these centuries later? The book is bound with the dried skin of Father Garnet.

If Father Garnet died for nothing, if there is no ultimate justice, then all that's left of him is a macabre book. If Father Garnet had no appeal to an ultimate justice, then the world does indeed make no sense.

Legs Don't Make the Man

There's a new school of atheists who trot out the old arguments. There is no God because there is no justice in this life, as if God creates man's inhumanity to man. They argue that the inequities of this world—that evil triumphs over good, that the poor never win, that humans suffer without regard to merit or guilt— prove a nonexistent God. No God worthy of worship could allow evil to persist so victoriously, they say.

Yeah, well, life makes even less sense if there is no God and if there is no ultimate justice, no ultimate balance. Life becomes a nasty, brutish and short affair punctuated only by the occasional hilarity at the meaninglessness of it all. That's not it, and we know it in our bones. We know it in our nature, and we know it in what Dante described as the sure and certain knowledge that "that uncreated, ineffable first One, / has fashioned all that moves in mind and space / in such sublime proportions that no one / can see it and not feel His Presence there."[3] We know it in his justice.

The Old Man took me to see the New York Knicks at the first Madison Square Garden. This was so long ago that he could walk up to the gate to buy our tickets, and the Harlem Globetrotters were the top billing and the Knicks game almost an afterthought.

It was quite a trek down to New York City from our insulated suburban neighborhood in Yonkers. Right after the game I met my first panhandler. He was an old black fellow. His legs were missing from the knees down, so he pushed himself down the sidewalk in a handcart. He held out a paper cup and asked for some change. The Old Man gave me a couple of nickels to put in the cup.

"Knicks win?" the panhandler asked me.

"Yes, sir," I answered, trying not to stare at the legs that weren't there.

"Globetrotters more fun to watch?"

"Yes, sir," I said, and he laughed.

On the train back home, I told the Old Man that I couldn't imagine living without any legs. The Old Man said, "Legs don't make the man. You'd be surprised what you could live without."

They were debating whether or not to ban panhandling in Pittsburgh. The general consensus was that panhandlers intimidated downtown visitors and used whatever they collected for various addictions. Just about all the local churches and social service agencies spoke in favor of the ban. "Send them to us," the churches said, "not to a liquor store or their drug supplier."

The first time I came to downtown Pittsburgh with my wife, we met up with the "Shouter." A middle-aged woman, she stalked the streets purposefully, yelling out in the bluest of blue language her various complaints about the world. I was told that she showed up now and then when she had skipped her meds and that she was generally harmless.

Another local favorite was the "Flower Guy." His gimmick was to walk up to you with a sweet smile and hand you a flower. As soon as you took it, he began to badger you for money. He followed some people for blocks, calling them every name in the book if they didn't fork over a buck.

My personal favorite was the "Sad Sack." With the perennial look of the old clown Emmett Kelly, his shoulders drooping passively, Sad Sack would ask, "Just a little bit for a meal. I'm awfully hungry."

But if you tried to direct him to a soup kitchen, he would tell you all about his kidneys that were shot, leaving him with a very limited diet. "That costs money," he said—at a diner far, far away. You always got a seemingly heartfelt "God bless!" when you gave in.

If there is a sucker born every minute, I took up my apportioned time and more. Panhandlers look at me like a piece of rare steak and lick their chops. After hearing lectures from the guys who operate a nearby soup kitchen, I finally managed a "no" one time to Sad Sack and directed him their way. He countered with his kidneys, and I responded with an argument for soup and a sandwich.

When Sad Sack realized that I wasn't fooling this time, he looked at me as if I had told him his dog had died. He shrugged those droopy shoulders, turned and walked away. No "God bless!" this time.

To be honest, I hated myself for the rest of the day. I guess that giving to a panhandler had become an easy grace—a way to feel better about myself without really putting myself out at all. But on the other hand, I always think, in the words of Blessed Mother Teresa, that these guys are "Christ in his more distressing form."

On Eagles' Wings

I was spending a weekend with family and friends back in Indiana, where I lived a lot of years after graduating from the fairer fields of Fairfield University. Somebody suggested that we run out to the reservoir. They had found an eagles' nest, complete with Mom, Dad and Baby Eagle, high up in a tree. You could view the nest from a neighboring ledge without getting the occupants worked up.

I agreed to go because I'm agreeable. But in my heart of hearts, I believe nature should be left alone. Just as I believe nature should leave me alone.

The trek to the eagles' nest took us past the old softball field where I had made a fool of myself years ago trying to pretend that I was still a ballplayer, even though my glove had seen more summers than the kids I played against. We used to play softball in the shadow of a county home, the next-to-last stop for the indigent elderly. It was still operating back then, a ramshackle old house with ramshackle old occupants, mostly men. They were the guys whom time had forgotten. They had no funds, friends or family left, and they were living out their last days on the county dole. The staff of the home actually called them inmates rather than residents.

Sometimes a guy would wander down to the field. He'd quietly watch a game, and I often wondered if it brought back memories or was just another way to kill time. The old men never said anything, and they would sit on the bleachers until the powers-that-be came down to haul them back. "You know you are not allowed to walk off the grounds, so why did you do it?" Nurse Ratchet would say. Our group of thirty-and-under ballplayers would watch out of the corners of our eyes and swear that would never happen to us.

The county home is gone now, a victim of modern times and the wrecking ball. Ironically, it was replaced by spanking new softball fields, complete with lights for night games. My old field is looking pretty ratty, the fence down in parts and splotches of weeds in the dusty infield. Everything eventually goes to seed, including ball fields and ballplayers.

We wandered through the briars and brambles, across a few paths, then entered the woods. There a fenced area bore a little plaque stating that this was the site of the county home burial grounds. There are no tombstones, and the place is overgrown with trees, weeds, ivy and all the detritus of a woods reclaiming itself. I noted the plaque and asked my brother-in-law where they moved the bodies.

"They didn't move them," he answered, and he pointed to the depressions where the loose earth had sunk in. "They're still there."

I thought about old men living out their last days alone, dying alone and being buried alone. Now the woods have settled over them, and no marker can even give us a name if we want to say a prayer. So I said a prayer for all of them, wishing them God's eternal justice.

Mom and Dad Eagle didn't make it back to the nest while we were there. And Baby Eagle was more like Teen Eagle, perched on a branch above the nest and looking as if he were bursting to get out on his own. I wished him well. It can be a tough world out there.

The atheist argument is that there is no God because there is no justice in the world. Old men die alone, after all, and a beneficent God would not allow such a thing. And I wonder why we allow it and believe that if there is no God to give us perfect justice in the next life, then nothing really makes sense at all.

Dante used an eagle as a symbol of divine justice, an eagle consisting of the souls of all the great lawgivers now in heaven. He waxed poetic on this, and I'm not arguing with him.

> Those who regret that we die here on earth
> to live above, have never known the freshening
> downpour of God's eternal grace up here.[4]

Justice is the faith lived, no matter the conditions, no matter what appearance it might take on, no matter how the story ends in the human condition.

Leaving It All Behind

My father-in-law was nearing the end. We all knew it, though we didn't talk about it. He certainly knew it. Every day he let go of things a little bit more.

It was the final inventory people take when they are dying. Many of us have witnessed that final visit to things, people and events that have to be reviewed and then quietly dropped. It's like peeling away layers of winter clothing in front of a warm fireplace. They discard the stuff they've accumulated until there's nothing but them and God.

My father-in-law was not an introspective man and certainly not a self-absorbed kind of guy. He fought a war, married and raised kids, worked in a factory and played golf on the weekends. He enjoyed Christmas with his grandkids and a beer with his buddies down at the VFW. Any kind of interior conversation was confined to talking himself into a better three-wood from the fairway. But I really think he was doing that last inventory as he watched the world go by outside his window at the nursing home.

We had never expected the nursing home to provide his last bed. He had some troubles, the troubles got worse, and then it all unraveled. So just weeks before that last Thanksgiving, we were sitting at a desk registering him for the nursing home, wondering what truck had run us over.

The young woman across from us, taking down all the pertinent information, was dressed as the bride of Frankenstein. A nurse walked in sporting vampire teeth; another was a cowgirl. It was Halloween, which gave the scene just the kind of touch that it needed, if described by Kafka.

And now a few weeks later the kids were home for Thanksgiving. We planned to bring the whole shootin' match out to the nursing home—the turkey, pies, dressing, mashed potatoes and grandkids. We also had a new addition to the family, a big Labrador retriever that the kids had taken through the puppy stage at school as a gift for their mom. My father-in-law liked dogs, and we planned to introduce him.

The nursing home called Thanksgiving morning to say that Dad was having a bad day. Maybe we could visit later. So we hurried through Thanksgiving dinner at my mother-in-law's house.

People never seem to do what they should do at moments when everything is about to change. We want it all cloaked in normalcy. We headed out to the nursing home with a big dog in tow.

It wasn't much of a visit. My father-in-law was not in good shape, and we couldn't know if he even recognized us. We tried to show him the new dog, but there was no response, though I kept wondering what he might have thought of it all that he couldn't tell us.

He rallied later on in the night, once the staff could relieve the pain. My mother-in-law came back the next morning. She did some knitting while he watched golf on television. Then she looked up to say something to him, and he was gone.

It was OK. He was done with his inventory.

We had buried my Old Man seven years before on All Saints' Day. I try to remember them both every day.

> Then I saw a new heaven and a new earth; the first heaven and the first earth had passed away, and the sea was no more. And I saw the holy city, new Jerusalem, coming down out of heaven from God, prepared as a bride adorned for her husband; and I heard a great voice from the throne, saying, "Behold the dwelling of God is with men. He will dwell with them, and they shall be his people, and God himself will be with them; he will wipe away every tear from their eyes, and death shall be no more, neither shall there be mourning nor crying out nor pain, for the former things have passed away." (Revelation 21:1–4)

And in the End

A few of the guys from the hall spoke at the funeral of my friend's father, reminding those in attendance that he was a union man through and through, always had a kind word and a bad haircut and was a devout Catholic. One guy recalled how he would take them all into Pittsburgh on Fridays, arriving in time for the noon Mass at the church downtown.

The homeless in Pittsburgh got to know my friend's father as a guy who could never say no, and they would surround the van the moment it arrived. He would give handouts until he had no more to give, and the guys from the hall, grumbling about noon

Mass when it wasn't even Sunday, grumbled all the more as his generosity shamed them into opening their wallets.

One morning before they went into the city, they had a presentation at the hall from some organization. At the end of the bread and circuses, they all received new powder-blue union jackets. My friend's father packed them into the van, and they headed for downtown resplendent in their new jackets.

When they got out of the van, the homeless receded like a fast ebb tide, disappearing into wherever they went when it was time not to be seen. The union gang headed into church, their pockets a bit more filled than they had anticipated. But as my friend's father sat at Mass, he grew more and more anxious. Finally he got up and walked outside. He collared one of the homeless and asked why they took for the hills when they got out of the van.

"We saw them jackets," he explained, "and we thought it was government men."

After the funeral I really did know everything that was important about this father of a friend that I thought a stranger. After all, he had left Mass to find out what had happened to the homeless.

> O sacred head surrounded....
> I see thy strength and vigor
> All fading in the strife,
> And death with cruel rigor,
> Bereaving thee of life;
> O agony and dying!
> O love to sinners free!
> Jesus, all grace supplying,
> O turn thy face on me.

.

.

.

.

.

.

PART TWO

{The Theological Virtues}

Faith, hope and love, collectively, are called the theological virtues. They are different from the cardinal virtues in that they are gifts freely given by God. We don't buy them, learn them, teach them, give them or even emulate them. They come to us in the sanctifying grace of baptism, and we are called to them through the grace that surrounds us every day.

The theological virtues are, however, calls to action as well. We can grow in faith, hope and love, just as we can grow in prudence and the other cardinal virtues.

The theological virtues tell us that all life is anchored in God; they are our personal ties to the living God.

.

.

.

.

.

.

CHAPTER FIVE

{Faith}

Faith is "the free response of the human person to the initiative of God who reveals himself" (Catechism of the Catholic Church, 166). Faith is a gift of grace from God, never forced or imposed. Faith is not a blind leap but rather, since it is based in God and from God, belief with certainty. However, faith also requires us to grow in understanding of the truth. By its very nature faith demands that it be at the very core of our lives.

His name was Snuffy Stirnweiss, and that might ring a bell faintly with some New Yorkers older than I. Snuffy—given name George—was a second baseman for the New York Yankees during World War II and just after. The son of a New York police officer, he was exempt from the military because of chronic ulcers. He had been a star football player at North Carolina but took a flier on pro baseball. He was called up from the Newark Bears in 1943, when most of the Yankee regulars had been drafted.

But Stirnweiss was no substitute scrub. Hall-of-Fame Yankee manager Joe McCarthy called him one of the toughest competitors he ever saw, and Snuffy won the American League batting title in 1945. He survived the return of the first-stringers from the war and finished his career in the early 1950s with the Cleveland Indians, retiring at the age of thirty-three.

Snuffy entered the business world and, on September 18, 1958, was on Jersey Central Train 932 heading into New York. The motorman on 932 had a heart attack, and the train blew through two signals, then plunged off a bridge into a Jersey port. Snuffy was killed. His hand was still clutching a rosary when his body was found.

Every so often the Church will reaffirm an essential teaching: that the Church is the one, true Church of Jesus Christ. When it does so there are usually some catcalls from the sidelines. The essential complaint will be that the Church is claiming some kind of monopoly on religious truth. Yet there really shouldn't be backtracking on the essential point that the Church believes that Christ lives in the sacraments and that his truth persists fully and completely in the Church, even in this mushy age when acknowledgement of differences violates some vague notion of tolerance.

The whole thing gets down to faith and logic, not tolerance. I'm not going to ground my fundamental understanding of life in somebody's burp. I believe in the one, holy, catholic and apostolic Church. I don't believe in some guy's opinion of Christ. If the Catholic faith is simply a man-made conjecture, as good as some but not much better than others, then I'll be damned if I base my life on it.

"Mankind's greatest fear," a priest said to me once between a bite of cheeseburger and a slug of cold beer, "is that Jesus meant exactly what he said." Which was a pretty good observation, considering we were in an airport bar.

The one great unifying theme of contemporary Gnosticism—a whole popular culture of books and movies—is that Jesus did not rise from the dead. His bones are simply dust somewhere. The fear that permeates everything from the Gnostic gospel craze to authors and publishers desperate to make a buck off cheap anti-Catholic thrillers is that the story told in Scripture is so very true: Christ has died, Christ is risen, Christ will come again. So that is what they go after.

Fearful souls hope that his grave was not empty after all. They want a resurrection that isn't a resurrection, a Jesus who isn't what he said he is. It is fear, more than anything else, that forces a person to think around the Resurrection, to explain it away, to turn it into a mushy nothing rather than truth. Because if what the Scriptures tell us and what the Church has steadfastly believed for two thousand years is true—that Jesus rose from the dead—then those fearful souls can't go on the way they have gone on. Conversion becomes necessary.

I often think of Snuffy Stirnweiss and his rosary. I don't think Snuffy was grasping at an opinion when he clutched that rosary into eternity. His was an act of faith.

Pope John Paul the Great

The Holy Father sat at the window, looking out at the crowds gathered below to hear his Easter message. Lord knows, he tried. But all the crowd could hear were rasping breaths as he struggled, physically struggled, to speak.

Finally the microphone was pushed aside, and he blessed them with the Sign of the Cross, in the name of the Father, the Son and the Holy Spirit. He was dying. And in Vatican Square that day, many wept.

When Pope John Paul II was elected pope on October 16, 1978, many of the pundits wondered to whatever microphone would listen about the cultural blinders that a pope from Eastern Europe would bring with him, picturing to the media a Polish Church locked in a pre–Vatican II deep freeze with a fixation on a dated anti-Communism. The implication seemed to be that the new pope would need some education in the ways of the world. But it would be this Polish pope who would widen the picture and open us to the overarching questions of what it means to be human in the modern world.

This pope saw contemporary man in a new way: He saw humanity alone in a secular trap, not knowing the fundamental answers to the elementary questions: Who am I? Why am I here? What is the purpose of my life?

The result was fear: fear of the present, fear of the future.

George Weigel neatly summed up the pope's first message in his masterful biography of John Paul II, *Witness to Hope*: "The world, he reflected, was afraid of itself and of its future. To all those who were afraid, to all those caught in the great loneliness of the modern world, 'I ask you. . . I beg you, let Christ speak to [you]. He alone has words of life, yes, of eternal life.'"[1]

At the very beginning of his papacy, Pope John Paul II said, "Be not afraid." He was citing Jesus speaking to his apostles when he came among them after his Resurrection. Pope John Paul had this message for the world that day and for every day of his papacy: "Be not afraid to welcome Christ and accept his power.... Be not afraid. Christ knows 'what is in man.' He alone knows it."[2]

On March 15, 1979, the new Holy Father released the encyclical *Redemptor Hominis* ("The Redeemer of Man"). In this encyclical—an ode to Christ as the Savior and Light of the World—Pope John Paul II established the dramatic message of his papacy and the themes that would intertwine for the next twenty-six years. He described a world on the cusp of a new millennium, a celebration of the incarnation of Christ. Through the Incarnation God revealed himself to humanity and "gave human life the dimension that he intended man to have from his first beginning."[3]

Religious liberty is not merely one right among many but the fundamental right from which all other human rights evolve, the Holy Father explained, because it underlines the essential dignity of every human life that comes from the Creator. And when that essential dignity is recognized in religious expression, the petty tyrannies of life—whether imposed by a dictatorial government apparatchik or a philosophy of materialism that reduces man to a cog in the machine—vanishes.

The answer to mankind's restless quest is simple: God. God as revealed through the Incarnation. Weigel explains *Redemptor Hominis*:

> The answer to humanity's fear of itself lay in rediscovering that human nature is moral and spiritual, not simply material....
>
> John Paul concludes his inaugural encyclical by revisiting one of the most familiar sentences in St. Augustine's *Confessions*—"You have made us for yourself, Lord, and

our heart is restless until it rests in you." Here, he pro-
poses, is the key to unlocking the mystery of modern restlessness, modern fear, and the "insatiability" built into
modern materialism.... The restlessness of modern hearts
could be calmed, the hungers that burdened our souls
satisfied, and the fear that haunted the modern world dis-
pelled, if men and women shared in the prophetic,
priestly, and kingly missions of Christ—if they freely
grasped the truth, freely worshipped in the truth, and
freely served one another and the world in truth.[4]

It would be that fundamental message that Pope John Paul II
would carry worldwide in his pontificate. His call and message
was simple: a call to conversion, a call to know God. Everything
in our lives reflects our relationship with God. With God we
have all; without him we only have ourselves and the loneliness
and the fear.

I met the Holy Father once, for a brief handshake. It was during his second papal pilgrimage to the United States, in
September 1987. He was speaking in Los Angeles to leaders in
the communications field. The group in attendance were
Hollywood's A-list, and I felt not a bit presumptuous—and not a
little starstruck—being smack in the middle of just about every
star I could remember from too many hours spent in movie
houses and in front of a television set.

And then the Holy Father arrived, standing in front of this
group and addressing them about their vital need to actually
care about the implications their entertainment has for the
popular culture of America and the world. He got polite
applause but not much subsequent action.

His speech done, the pope walked slowly up the aisle, greeting the Hollywood A-list personally. They reached out to touch him, to whisper a few words, to smile (and not a few with tears in their eyes). I thought one famous starlet was going to collapse right in front of him as she asked for his blessing.

As I leaned across and he grasped my hand, I could only say, "Thank you, Holy Father. Thank you for everything." He looked at me for a few short seconds, then he smiled, nodded his head and moved on to the next jelly-legged starlet.

The news came to the crowds assembled in Vatican Square that the Holy Father had died. The tears began in earnest then, flowing all over the world. But I remembered another crowd in the first year of his papacy: a million of his fellow Poles, still in the grip of Soviet autonomy and the puppetlike tyranny of their imposed Communist government, gathered in Victory Square in Warsaw to hear his message. As he spoke to them of Jesus, from somewhere in the crowd a chant began that would soon come from every voice: "We want God!" they said over and over again. "We want God!"

A Little Scripture

As John the Evangelist tells the story, the apostles were gathered together "on the evening of that...first day of the week" (John 20:19). They were frightened. Jesus had been crucified, and no one knew if the soldiers would come for them next. But stranger still, women had returned from the site of his burial and told them of an empty tomb.

Peter and another disciple had run to the place where Joseph of Arimathea and Nicodemus had laid the body. The one disciple arrived before Peter, peered into the tomb and saw discarded burial cloths. Nervous, he could not go in. He waited for the slower Peter to arrive, and they entered the tomb together. They saw the discarded burial cloths. And they saw the cloth that had wrapped the head of Jesus, folded neatly and set off to one side. They did not know what to think, and they returned home to tell the others.

Mary of Magdala had stayed behind. The horror of the death of Jesus, and now the missing body, had left her devastated. Crying, she looked again into the tomb. And she saw two men—angels, she was certain—at the head and foot of the tomb. They asked her why she was crying. She told them that someone had taken away the body of Jesus, and she did not know where to find him.

Turning to leave, she saw another man standing there. He also asked her why she cried. Thinking him a gardener, she begged him to tell her where he had moved the body of Jesus. And he answered her by name: "Mary." He told her to go to the disciples and tell them, "I am going to my Father and your Father, to my God and your God." She ran to the disciples and told them, "I have seen the Lord" (see John 20:1–18).

So they huddled together behind locked doors, trying to make sense of all that had happened: their Last Supper together, the arrest in the garden, the trial, the way of the cross, the crucifixion, the death. They had seen it all, and now they had word of an empty tomb and Mary's astounding message.

And then, "Peace be with you," he said. This was no apparition. Jesus stood there, and he showed them his hands and his side lanced at the crucifixion. He was alive. He had risen from the dead. He said to them again, "Peace be with you." Then he gave them their mission: "As the Father has sent me, even so I send you." Breathing on them, he said to them: "Receive the Holy Spirit. If you forgive the sins of any, they are forgiven; if you retain the sins of any, they are retained" (John 20:19–23).

One of the apostles, Thomas, was not in that room that evening. When the apostles told him that Jesus was alive, he scoffed. "Unless I see in his hands the print of the nails, and place my finger in the marks of the nails, and place my hand in his side, I will not believe" (John 20:25).

A week later the disciples were gathered again in the same room, Thomas with them. And Jesus came again, stood among them and said, "Peace be with you." Then he turned to Thomas, offering his hands and side so that the apostle might believe. Thomas fell to his knees, saying, "My Lord and my God!" Jesus answered, "You have believed because you have seen me. Blessed are those who have not seen and yet believe" (John 20:26–29).

Jesus offered them peace, to end their fear. He appeared again so that Thomas would believe. And he promised faith to all who have not seen but believe.

A Christmas Story
It was one of those little moments. But the faith is always taught in the little moments.

My daughter was visiting just after Thanksgiving. Her husband had suggested that she take a little time with her folks, as she was already getting a bad case of cabin fever since she had stopped working. Nearing the sixth month of her pregnancy, my little girl planned on making us the grandparents of twins before opening day of the baseball season.

As I looked at her at the beginning of Advent—those days of holy anticipation for Christmas—I decided that she might not make it to the time pitchers and catchers report. She was help-ing us decorate the house for Christmas. No heavy lifting, just unwrapping this and that of the Christmas gewgaws I had hauled down in boxes from the attic.

I am not one who fights the "commercialization of Christmas." A few years back there was a story on the holiday songs that got the most play over the radio. It was pretty much a washout for religious tunes. Number one was Nat King Cole's "The Christmas Song," the one about chestnuts roasting on an open fire. Rounding out the top five were the Pretenders' rendition of "Have Yourself a Merry Little Christmas," "Winter Wonderland" by Eurythmics, "Santa Claus Is Coming to Town" by Bruce Springsteen and that old favorite, Bing Crosby's "White Christmas." The only distinctly religious tune to make the list was "The Little Drummer Boy," which gives me a headache.

As we were passing around the list by e-mail and swapping rude comments, one friend brought a little sense to the conver-sation when he wrote that he always found "The Christmas Song" to be profoundly religious and incarnational. Tweaking the song of Shadrach, Meshach and Abednego from the third chapter of the book of Daniel, he told us:

> Chestnuts and frost, bless the Lord!
> Carols and winter wardrobe, bless the Lord!
> Turkey and mistletoe, bless the Lord!

"Christmas," he concluded, "marks the elevation of all these things of nature."

Most of the symbols of Christmas are rooted in the spiritual nature of the feast. Despite the orgy of consumerism and the trend toward winter solstice celebrations, nobody can get around the fact that all the hoopla is rooted in the birth of Christ. It is not just in Nativity scenes, crowded churches and faith-based carols sung over the radio. It's also in Elvis Presley warbling through a blue Christmas, lights covering houses, evergreens tied to the tops of cars and soon to be decorated with ornaments crafted in third-grade classrooms, kids crying on Santa Claus's lap at the mall, picking out the tie for Uncle Joe or the perfume for Aunt Betty and "Jack Frost nipping at your nose."

Christmas is a thousand images blessed by time and memory. It's a time of year when every story celebrates conversion and faith rewarded, the sense that miracles can happen. There is even a secular need for Something to happen that will change lives and continue the brightness anticipated with colored lights and angels on top of trees.

The unspoken miracle that everyone hopes for at Christmas is really very simple: a conversion, or reversion, to a life centered in the faith celebrated in the season. If that's recognized and pursued, the light and joy remain after the tree is hauled away. And they remain for an eternity.

Grace builds on nature, we tell ourselves. There is no better proof of that than Christmastime in America.

I was raised a Christmas Eve guy. With an Irish sense of the liturgical cycle, my mother wouldn't allow more than a hint of Christmas around the house until Christmas Eve. That night, after the Old Man came home from work, we'd have a three-hour marathon that turned the house into a Christmas paradise. The tree would be dragged in from the porch and decorated with a family's worth of trinkets and colored lights, everything from the paper Santa my brother had made in third grade to the tinsel that we'd still be picking out of the carpet come Easter. Gifts wrapped in secret came out of the closets, and stockings were hung in anticipation.

The final touch would be putting up the crèche on the mantelpiece. This was no family heirloom, probably just something my mother picked up at a W.T. Grant's sale one January. But we liked it, and as with so many Christmas customs, tradition ruled how it was to be arranged. Every figure had its place, from Mary and Joseph in the stable to the wise men at the far side of the mantelpiece, to be moved ever so slowly each day after Christmas, arriving in front of the Christ Child on the Feast of the Epiphany.

The Christ Child figure would be put aside that night, to appear in the stable on Christmas morning. This was one way— a very simple way—for my parents to help keep the true meaning of Christmas clear in our house.

When my son and daughter were growing up, I quickly caved on the Christmas Eve decorating. The age of artificial trees jacked up the peer pressure, and each year we would bargain over how many days before Christmas the tree could take its place in the living room. But one custom remained. My daughter, the traditional arranger of the crèche, would put the Christ Child aside each year. And every Christmas morning, an unshaven, disheveled dad would not call out to the kids that Christmas had come until the Christ Child had been placed in its sacred spot, to help keep the meaning of Christmas clear in our house.

So now we were decorating the house right after Thanksgiving weekend, only because my daughter was there to help. I was digging into a bag of colored bulbs, wondering what we did with the tree topper, when I noticed that she was putting the finishing touches on our family crèche. When she unwrapped the Christ figurine—from the crèche of her childhood—she carried it over to the china hutch and placed it inside, where it would rest until Christmas morning.

Smiling at my daughter, so alive with her children to be, I knew that the meaning of Christmas would be clear in her house for a new generation. Because the faith is always taught in the little moments.

Peanuts *and More*

The curious thing about reading Dante today is how the faith is presumed. Dante wrote in an age before the Reformation. While he condemned to hell and purgatory a host of his Italian enemies—popes, bishops and priests—the basics of the faith were presumed. He castigated political opponents, not religious perspectives. Even the heretics punished in his *Inferno* were there for foolishness more than abject heresy. The faith was the ordinary and assumed. The faith was there for all to see.

> Do not be like a feather in the wind,
> or think that every water washes clean!
>
> You have the Testaments, the Old and New;
> as guide you have the Shepherd of the church:
> they should be all you need to save your soul.[5]

While on his pilgrimage through paradise, Dante was quizzed like a catechism student by the apostles Peter, James and John on his understanding of faith, hope and love. For his definition of faith Dante responded to Saint Peter:

> Faith is the substance of those hoped-for things
> and argument for things we have not seen....

> ... The deep mysteries of Heaven
> that generously reveal themselves to me
> are so concealed from man's eyes down on earth
>
> that they exist there only in belief.[6]

The PBS *American Masters* portrait of Charles Schulz, the cartoonist who created *Peanuts*, included snippets from an interview Schultz had given on *The Today Show* as his comic strip was concluding. Schultz was dying of cancer, and in fact, he would die the day before the last original strip appeared. Schultz was asked about one of the ongoing gags of the strip, where Lucy would always pull the football away just as Charlie Brown was about to kick it.

At one time Schultz had said that he could never let Charlie Brown kick that ball. "That would be a terrible disservice to him after nearly half a century." But in this interview shortly before his death, he asked slowly, "Why didn't I ever let that little kid kick the ball?" as if he couldn't understand this at all. And then he was quiet, looking down and away from the camera.

It broke my heart.

We're reminded of Schultz every December when *A Charlie Brown Christmas* airs. The twenty-five-minute show was first broadcast on December 9, 1965, preempting a broadcast of *The Munsters*. The show involves Charlie Brown's search for the real meaning of Christmas in a world of commercialism. The *Peanuts* gang gets the answer when Linus recites the Nativity narrative from Luke. The show ends with all the kids joining together for a chorus of "Hark! The Herald Angels Sing."

What surprised me was that even back in 1965, the producers wanted to eliminate Linus's Bible reading. They feared it would offend people, that it would be too "preachy" for a children's broadcast and people wouldn't sit through it. Schultz, a Sunday school teacher, insisted that the Nativity narrative remain. It's good that he won the argument, as it became the lynchpin of the whole show. Without that reading, which one critic at the time called "the dramatic highlight of the season," *A Charlie Brown Christmas* would have been essentially meaningless.

It is said that Schultz abandoned his religious faith. In the late 1980s he allegedly said, "I do not go to church anymore.... I guess you might say I've come around to secular humanism, an obligation I believe all humans have to others and the world we live in."[7] Which sets up a ridiculous dichotomy between religious faith and service to humanity. Schultz was smarter than that.

I prefer to believe that Schultz "fought the good fight" (2 Timothy 4:7) to the end. Only a believer could be so upset because he never let good ol' Charlie Brown kick that ball.

A Natural Hubris

I had wheedled the Old Man into letting me have a paper route. Paper routes were like dogs. Fathers got nervous about them because they would always end up their responsibility. It would be the Old Man stuck with walking the dog at midnight and doing the paper route during a snowstorm. It's part of the job description for fatherhood.

But he let me have the route anyway, and on that first day I was waiting as the truck delivered the Yonkers afternoon daily in a fat bundle. I diligently counted each of the sixty-three papers that were my responsibility and placed them in the white canvas bag that came with the job. I strapped the load around my shoulder, stood up and promptly flipped right over the bag.

I weighed all of about seventy pounds, so the full bag of papers was more than I could lift. I could only deliver about half the papers at a time, then backtrack to pick up the rest. The horrible point in all this is that when my older sister offered to help one day, she stuffed all the papers in the bag and picked it up as daintily as a cup of tea.

I learned a lot on that paper route, including the surprising fact that adults would stiff a kid for a crummy four bits and that small dogs and trained parrots are far more terrifying than you would think. Those lessons have served me well in life.

The one customer I dreaded on the route was a lady from our parish, Mrs. Barcatolli. We all knew her. During Mass she would say the rosary while going from one Station of the Cross to the next. She gave me holy cards instead of tips, once asked me to kneel to pray with her right on her front porch and berated me for delivering the paper on Ascension Thursday. "You should have quit before working on a holy day of obligation!" she shouted.

The pastor told me not to worry about it. She had "scruples," he said, and my mother told me that meant she would confess to biting her fingernails on a meatless Friday.

The thesis is that people today have a need for "sense" and "meaning" in their lives, but they are lost because they no longer believe in truth, particularly religious truth. In the past, the theory goes, people were often believers without belonging. They accepted the basic principles of their faith but didn't bother to practice the faith—out of sheer laziness or contrariness. Today, the theory goes, religious doubt is the new intellectual standard.

People propose that there is no truth, at least a truth that can be known. But that leaves them with no answers to life's fundamental questions. Because without truth there are no answers. This is called postmodern cognitive dissonance or something like that. People want to belong, but they can't convince themselves to believe.

Hubris used to mean a pride in knowledge, man thinking that he could basically reason to all truths without need of divine revelation. Today we have a hubris of ignorance, a pride in the belief that the fundamental truth is that there is no truth.

It is a new spin on poor Mrs. Barcatolli's scruples. She lived in terror of a hundred transgressions a day, paralyzed in the minutiae of sin. Today's agnostics are similarly victims. They believe that there is no knowable truth. And they believe that to be the truth. It's a postmodern cultural trap, an intellectual catch-22.

Doubt will always exist. It comes with the territory this side of creation. That's why the faith is a pilgrimage, never an end point. But building your life on doubt will get you nowhere.

Wearing the Faith

I was sitting at a booth in a greasy spoon where an old feller was telling a story to his friends. His hearing was probably going, because anybody could catch every word even if working back in the kitchen. Old men shout their conversations when the ears go on them.

"So I was visiting my son-in-law, and there was his beagle, looking pretty sharp. So I said, 'The old dog looks good.' And he said, 'I just gave him a haircut.'

"'You cut hair?' I ask him. And he says, 'The beagle's.' And I say, 'Good enough for me; how about giving me a cut?' And he says, 'Sure.'

"So he gives me the haircut and says, 'What do you think?' I look in the mirror, look at the beagle and say, 'The dog looks better.'"

And everybody in for morning coffee and eggs—friend or stranger—gave a chuckle.

I see these old fellers in different places. Two retired guys walk together in the neighborhood as I head out for work at the cusp of sunrise. Four of them never sit together in the same pew at morning Mass, but they meet on the steps of the church afterward to swap a few observations on life, death and the National Football League. And a few of them sit together with the old feller at the little restaurant and tell stories about when they were working. They tease the waitress, who teases them back, and they leave her a good tip because she makes their day a little brighter just by being pretty.

I admire the company of men post-seventy. A certain relaxation seems to catch up with them, even though the insurance guys figure that they are as likely to drop from a big one as to get out of bed in the morning. But it's not that they stop caring about living; they just stop worrying about it.

The faith seems to come naturally to them. They live it and wear it like an old flannel shirt.

Nurtured on a lifetime of the sacraments, they find that grace has become an old friend.

A sidebar to the story about Snuffy Stirnweiss: The number of the train that crashed was "932," and it appeared in all the news reports and in pictures in the paper. A lot of people took it as an omen and played that number in the bookie lotteries popular at the time in the underground economy. And the number came in.

Most of the New York bookies were cleaned out. The papers reported that only "Newsboy" Moriarty had enough cash to cover his bets.

You've got to have faith.

.

.

.

.

.

.

.

CHAPTER SIX

{Hope}

The theological virtue of hope, a gift of God, is the certainty that if humanity is faithful to God, God will be faithful to humanity. Hope is not mere wishing but the serene and full confidence that God will never abandon us, no matter what this life gives or takes from us. It is firmness in faith that eternal life can be achieved and that the grace of God can overcome any obstacle in achieving that eternal life. Hope is at the heart of our faith.

I was probably about five years old when I had my first face-to-face experience with the death of someone I knew. She was a little old lady, the grandmother of one of my mother's friends. She lived in downtown Yonkers.

Every once in a while the Old Man drove my mother's friend downtown to see her grandmother. It was usually on a Sunday, and I'd tag along—with nothing better to do back in a time when every store closed on the Christian Sabbath and the family just waited around for a mid-afternoon supper.

We would usually spot the grandmother as she walked up the hill, heading home from Mass. A hat on her head and dressed to the nines, she was as bowlegged as a cartoon cowboy.

She'd climb in the car and give me a big hello. You know the rest: how I was cute as a button, had dimples the girls would just love, must have grown two inches since last week. Then she'd proceed to pinch my cheek and steal my nose, thumb squeezed between her knuckles. It was a ritual as strictly followed as the liturgy of the Latin Mass she attended.

She was an old-school Catholic: daily Mass, weekly confession, Rosary Altar Society, in the first pew at everything from Benediction to the Stations of the Cross during Lent. Her life was her faith, and her faith was her life.

And then she up and died. This being the 1950s and all, my mother explained that I wouldn't see her anymore, as she was now part of the eternal celestial choir. I couldn't imagine that. So I asked my mother if her church would still be around if she wasn't going to be there for Mass. Maybe I figured they would have to close up shop without her, now that she was working full-time in the eternal celestial choir. The church will always be there, my mother answered.

A month or so later, we were driving through her old neighborhood on a Sunday and went by her old church. Mass was just getting out, but I didn't see the old grandmother walking up the hill from the church. She really was gone.

And I began to understand. My mother had explained to me that the Church would always be there. Over the years I have come to know exactly what she meant.

Familiar Places

It's the little things that I try to hold on to. Maybe it's common to the human condition, the search for the familiar. A place gets comfortable, and when it's no longer there, it's as if a little piece of the heart goes with it. "Don't it always seem to go that you don't know what you've got till it's gone," Joni Mitchell sang in "Big Yellow Taxi."

When I was in high school, we gathered at a place called Louie's before class. It was under the elevated train platform that would take the movers and shakers into Manhattan from the Bronx. Louie's served fountain drinks and day-old donuts. The smoke was so thick from high school kids wanting to look older that a customer could barely see the back booths from the front door.

We drank our sodas, smoked our Luckies and put dimes in the jukebox. A buddy of mine got tossed out by Louie himself after playing "Wooly Bully" by Sam the Sham and the Pharaohs five times straight.

They had a little joint in the town where I live now, and I had grown accustomed to its face. It had gotten to the point that my wife was downright sick of it, so I only went when I was on my own. I liked it because I could have my own booth, I had the menu memorized, and all the waitresses knew the old geezer who overtipped for a sandwich and a cup of soup. I'd bring in a book and read a few pages while the hostess and the waitresses compared notes, watching the television over the bar if things were slow.

And things were usually slow, which should have let me know that they were going to pave paradise. I pulled up one night, and the little restaurant was locked up tight. A sign told the story:

"Commercial Property Available."

A few weeks later I was at one of those chain restaurants with the wife where they put peanuts in a bucket on your table and all the kids are so swell and cheerful serving overpriced meals. I spotted one of the waitresses who had worked at the old place. She gave me a little wave of recognition as she headed over with the other help to sing happy birthday to some poor schmuck at another table. I wanted to tell her to get out before she lost her soul. Instead I waved back sappily. So it goes.

Saint Augustine told us that we are all pilgrims and ever restless until we've finished the journey. I think sometimes that the very human longing for the familiar is part of that hope. And we always find out that the familiar in this life never lasts. That's a gift that only comes with eternal life.

When Cardinal Joseph Bernardin of Chicago was dying, he wrote that people would always ask him what heaven will be like. He remembered the first time that he visited the little town where his parents came from in Italy. Because he had seen so many pictures and heard so many descriptions, it was all familiar to him when he finally saw it in person. He felt that he was home. And he believed that heaven would be like that.

I try to remember Teresa of Avila's words: "Let nothing disturb you. Let nothing frighten you. All things pass. God does not change."[1]

Children of Men

I am at that odd point in life: I was a son; I am a father; I have become a grandfather. The hopes of three generations are mixed together.

A guy has his fantasies about what his son will be when he grows up. A buddy of mine, a writer, told me that he always imagined a son who would share his love for literature. His kid was a basketball star, but the attraction of the game was lost on the father. He just wanted to talk Shakespeare, while his kid shot baskets in the driveway.

My Old Man told me that just before I got married, something woke him up in the middle of the night back home in Yonkers. He got out of bed, looked out the window and swore he saw a seven-year-old me playing ball against the side of the house. My mother rolled over and asked him what he was doing. He told her what he saw, and she told him to come back to bed.

I was twenty-three then, and I thought the story meant that the Old Man was getting a little goofy as he neared retirement. It's one of those little stories that I hold on to now.

I try not to pull the grandfather rank with my daughter, her husband and her twin boys. The last thing they need is any advice from an old soldier who did his own battle with twins decades ago. The only thing I ever offer is that they cherish every second they have. Babies go away forever, and little boys soon enough.

The basic plot of the movie *Children of Men*, set in the year 2027, is that it has been eighteen years since the last baby was born anywhere in the world. "As the sound of the playground faded," a character explains, "the despair set in. Very odd, what happens in a world without children's voices."

That's what you have to watch out for as you get older. If you are not careful, you can slip into a world without the voices of children, and the despair can set in. That's why God allows us to become grandparents—so we can see children as children and not have to think about what they will be as grown-ups. That's their parents' job.

One by one my own dreams for glory have gone down the usual paths. I have no complaints. I had more blessings than I deserved. As the main character in the old Catholic novel *Mr. Blue* described himself, "Never was there a worse sinner, / And never was God kinder to one."[2]

But I wanted something more for my son. There was all the usual stuff, the yearnings of middle-aged men for what they never were and could no longer be. He played football and baseball, and I wanted him to be the kid who would grab all the headlines. I envisioned him at the top of his class in academics, even though his father had managed a stunningly consistent mediocrity in his own schoolwork.

As he served at the altar, I wondered if he would be a priest—a priest who would be one of the talking heads when the media wanted a Catholic explanation or one of those whom the girls would call "Father What-a-Waste," a ruggedly good-looking fellow with the pastoral élan of Bing Crosby in *Going My Way*.

I'd dream that we'd stay up late arguing my favorite topics in history and philosophy. We would wander through the intricacies of existentialism or the rise of nationalism in the nineteenth century, just for the fun of talking, thinking and discussing. We'd talk about the Great Books until dawn and go out for coffee and eggs at a greasy spoon.

Then the kid would go on to a life of great accomplishment—in athletics, law, medicine, business, maybe politics. And I'd walk down the street, and the neighbors would say, "There goes his father. He did a good job with that kid."

In one of the classic *Seinfeld* episodes, sad-sack George recalled how his father had invented "Festivus" as a replacement for Christmas. A highlight of the Festivus ritual was the annual review of how much George had disappointed him in the last year. Most of us are not as obvious as George's father. When our sons fail to meet the impossible expectations that we created for them, we keep it to ourselves. We are used to dreams fading away. It happens to us every day.

I was at the airport to pick up my son around the holidays. He was coming home for his first visit in a while. They make you wait in the terminal, as if an overweight, slightly more than middle-aged man is going to cause any trouble. So I was looking for him, straining along with everyone else to spot their loved ones coming home. I saw him before he saw me, so I could watch him unobserved for just a moment or two.

He was wearing the crisp, creased uniform of the United States Army. He had joined up, much to his father's horror, at the age of twenty-six. What kind of kid goes into the military when he is no longer a kid? I spent four years in college praying I would never get drafted. What did I know about the military? That's not a road I ever traveled or wanted for myself, nor for my son.

But there he was, all grown up and doing a masterful job of it. Better than his Old Man ever imagined.

"A dragon lives forever, but not so little boys," Peter, Paul and Mary sang when I was a kid in eighth grade. I liked "Puff the Magic Dragon" back then, not even realizing that it was a song about my buddies and me, just about to give up "painted wings and giant rings" to "make way for other toys."

Over the door of my old grammar school in Yonkers, there was a Scripture quote in big block letters: "Let the little children come to me" (Matthew 19:14). I passed under that every school day for eight years.

And then I grew up. I wonder if the Old Man ever forgave me.

A Little Scripture

After Dante was quizzed in paradise by Saint Peter on the meaning of faith, Saint James the apostle took over. He asked Dante what he believed hope to be.

> ...Hope
>
> is sure expectancy of future bliss
> to be inherited—the holy fruit
> of God's own grace and man's precedent worth....
>
> "Let them have hope in Thee who know Thy name,"
> so sings his sacred song. And who does not
> know of That Name if he has faith like mine?[3]

Lazarus, the brother of Martha and Mary, was dying (see John 11:1—44). The family sent word to Jesus that he must come to Bethany. He told his apostles that Lazarus had already died, but "for your sake I am glad that I was not there, so that you may believe. But let us go to him."

When they arrived Lazarus was already buried—four days in the tomb. Martha met Jesus, and she even took him to task. "Lord, if you had been here, my brother would not have died. And even now I know that whatever you ask from God, God will give you."

Jesus said simply, "Your brother will rise."

Martha responded that she knew he would rise on the day of resurrection. But then Jesus told her, "I am the resurrection and the life; he who believes in me, though he die, yet shall he live, and whoever lives and believes in me shall never die."

He asked Martha if she believed this, and she responded: "Yes, Lord; I believe that you are the Christ, the Son of God, he who is coming into the world."

They were joined by Mary, who was crying over the death of her brother. Jesus cried with her, then asked to be taken to the tomb. He ordered the stone rolled back, and Martha said that it should not be done, as the body would surely smell of death. Jesus said that he had promised her that she would see the glory of God, and then he prayed. He shouted: "Lazarus, come out."

Still wrapped in the burial cloths, Lazarus emerged alive. "Unbind him," Jesus said simply, "and let him go."

Saint Paul defined our hope simply:

> Now if Christ is preached as raised from the dead, how can some of you say that there is no resurrection of the dead? But if there is no resurrection of the dead, then Christ has not been raised; and if Christ has not been raised, then our preaching is in vain and your faith is in vain.... For if the dead are not raised, then Christ has not been raised. If Christ has not been raised, your faith is futile and you are still in your sins. Then those also who have fallen asleep in Christ have perished. If for this life only we have hoped in Christ, we are of all men the most to be pitied. (1 Corinthians 15:12–14, 16–19)

Pope Benedict XVI, citing Zechariah, described believers as "prisoners of hope." He wrote in his encyclical on hope, "The dark door of time, of the future, has been thrown open. The one who has hope lives differently; the one who hopes has been granted the gift of a new life."4

Believers share a common hope in God and in God's mercy. And a common hope in eternal life.

Jesus May Be Coming in the Morning

The woman sitting next to me on a fully packed airplane had a small blue mask to cover her mouth. It was one of those masks you saw the television doctor slip on just before the operation. I wondered if I had neglected to put on deodorant that morning. I was traveling on a Saturday, and I tend to relax some of the house rules on the weekend.

"I had a heart transplant," she said, making me think she had read my thoughts, "and have to be careful about things."

She was part of a national group of black Pentecostal women meeting in the same city where I had business. They had been everywhere downtown. You noticed them right away because they were dressed impeccably morning, noon and night for their meetings and services. Full evening gowns all the time but in the traditional sense: nothing slinky or strapless, just classy all the way.

They topped it all with hats of every conceivable size and style. The plane was at least half-filled with these women from the Pentecostal convention, and the overhead bins were packed with huge, round and decorated hatboxes such as I hadn't seen since peeking in my grandmother's closet. I thought no one wore hats like that anymore. They reminded me of Easter Sunday when I was a kid. Only the finest and fanciest of hats would make it to that Mass.

Back in my Hoosier parish, there was an elderly couple I saw at Mass all the time. He always wore a perfectly pressed blue suit, white shirt, tie and matching handkerchief carefully folded in the breast pocket. She always had on a sensible woman's suit, black short-heeled shoes and a small hat. Nobody else dressed like that for Mass unless they had somewhere to go after it was over.

The woman next to me on the plane went into a detailed account of the trouble that led to her transplant, at each point carefully thanking Jesus. The donor heart was from a young white male killed in a car accident, and she had become very close to the boy's mother, praise Jesus. She said that she told her personal story everywhere to encourage black people to donate organs. "Many of us worry that if we sign an organ donor card they'll just let us die for our parts," she said.

We talked a bit more, then settled into the usual quiet lassitude of a flight. I read a book, and she did a word puzzle based on the New Testament.

One of the women began to sing softly. The others joined in just as softly. I didn't quite get it, but it was something like

> Say a prayer tonight,
>   for Jesus may be coming in the morning.
> Say a prayer this morning,
>   for Jesus may be coming at noon;
> Say a prayer at noon,
>   for Jesus may be coming in the evening.

The plane was quiet as they sang and quiet as they finished in an almost whispered unison. It was the first time I had heard a spontaneous hymn at twenty thousand feet or so.

"I hope you will not be upset, but my faith tells me that I have to evangelize," my neighbor said to me toward the end of the flight. She reached into her bag and pulled out a little pamphlet titled "I Must Tell You This." The basic message was to say yes to Jesus. A few hairpins slipped out with the pamphlet, and I scooped them up and gave them back to her

I said, "I'm a churchgoer myself—a Catholic."

"That's a good thing," she said but didn't offer to take the pamphlet back.

When the plane landed there was a quick prayer of thanks to Jesus for seeing us all home safely... followed by a mighty struggle to dislodge the hatboxes.

Hope Among Strangers

My wife and I were in a little eatery outside Detroit, one of those places started by Great-Grandma and still run by the family. Everyone from the cook to the cashier girl to the busboy looks alike. A couple of bucks still buys coffee with bacon, eggs, potatoes and toast. Thrown in for free is a slice of the town you are visiting.

It was a Saturday morning, and two women of a certain age were bantering back and forth in the booth directly in back of us. I didn't mean to eavesdrop, but it was another one of those conversations that people force on you when they are a little hard of hearing.

It seemed that one of them was heading off on her first European trip, and she was getting scared. Her lady friend was warning her about the dangers of pickpockets and the incomprehensibility of the exchange system, adding that her ignorance of the native tongue would leave her open to all kinds of unsavory characters. She finally concluded: "Well, what's the worst that can happen? You come home in a casket." I didn't catch her friend's response.

Later that day I was hanging around outside a hospital, getting a few moments of fresh air before visiting the sick. Hospitals are a chore for everyone—workers, visitors, doctors and nurses. And worst of all for the patients, suffering through that terrible combination of boredom and fear.

A guy came out, a young fellow who didn't look much over thirty-five. He was lugging his whole setup with him—some kind of attached gizmo that was monitoring who knows what. He was in his pajamas and a robe and was escaping for a smoke. It was unseasonably and unreasonably warm for Detroit at the end of January.

"I asked my girlfriend to bring me some smokes yesterday," he said. "She brought four. I asked her why she didn't bring me a pack. She said she thought she'd get in trouble bringing smokes into a hospital." He followed with a look of exasperation.

Frankly, I thought she had a point—or an excuse. After all, there was a reason the guy was in the hospital, and I didn't think smoking was going to help the matter. I didn't ask what he was in for, but he volunteered that he was looking at surgery in the morning.

We chatted about the upcoming Super Bowl and the season the Pistons were having. He was smoking in quick bursts, savoring nothing. He was a guy who wanted the next twenty-four hours gone as soon as possible but the morning to never come.

It was time for me to go back in. He asked what I was there for. Just visiting, I answered, and he looked at me as if I were the luckiest guy alive. I told him good-bye, God bless and I'd say a prayer for him. He seemed to appreciate the offer, though a couple of smokes might have been more gratefully received.

The pilgrimage ends only once, whether it's a young guy looking at surgery in the morning or an elderly woman facing a trip that makes her more nervous with each approaching day. I hope she forgot her friend's advice and had the time of her life. I hope he had his surgery and, in the euphoria of survival, decided to make the rest of the pilgrimage smokeless.

We never know the battles people are waging. But we know that everyone has them and that everyone has to have hope. That's why we need to keep praying for each other. Especially the strangers.

Cheerios in Church

The church had a rack in the back, and I'm the kind of guy who peruses pamphlet racks. So while a handful of people knelt quietly and one woman lit a candle, I thumbed through the reading material.

A good friend's eighty-six-year-old father-in-law had passed away unexpectedly. You might want to make the argument that no death is unexpected at eighty-six, but he was a spry old feller, one of those blue-collar guys who knew nothing but working every day of his life. He kept busy until the very end. And then his daughter found him collapsed and gone on an Advent morning.

I was there for the funeral Mass, arriving early because the traffic from downtown to one of the old neighborhoods by the river is anybody's guess. An old Pittsburgh adage is that a trip can take fifteen minutes or forty-five, so people are usually fashionably late or uncomfortably early.

They brought the old guy back to the old neighborhood for the funeral Mass, the same church where they had the same Mass around a year before for his wife. They both lived with their daughter—my friend's wife—in another town but wanted to come home that last time.

It's a neighborhood that went through the change a few decades back, a story told many times over in southwestern Pennsylvania. The steel mills closed, and the jobs disappeared, creating an economic diaspora that hasn't ended yet. In the old neighborhoods, where today's great-grandmothers played as little girls, the windows are broken and the front doors nailed shut. In a lot of neighborhoods, the churches are the only things remaining, and their days could be numbered too.

The pamphlets in the church rack reflected the population. Half of them had to do with death and mourning, written for people who see a lot of funerals. This church serves the remnant, I thought, the last few who haven't gotten out of Dodge in time.

I put down a pamphlet as I noticed the choir beginning to take their seats. The hearse pulled up as close to the doors of the vestibule as possible, it being a cold, overcast and wet December morning. As if there are any other kinds of days that time of year in southwestern Pennsylvania.

As the family gathered around to accompany the casket into the church, I went to sit down. I had the pick of the pews. It was an old man's funeral on a Monday in the old neighborhood. Once the family had taken their seats, more than three-quarters of the church was still empty.

The priest did a good job of it: said all the right things in the homily, brought every consolation of the faith to the bereaved. The daughter gave a brief eulogy for her father when the Mass ended: hardworking, served in World War II, lived for his family, took care of his wife in her final illness, loved his grandchildren and his great-grandchildren. It could apply to a whole generation raised in that old neighborhood. But the story is fresh no matter how often the tale is told. A final commendation, and then the casket was taken out. I stood to watch the silent procession.

Something caught my eye in the pew in front of me. It was a Cheerio, a remnant from Sunday Mass that the ushers had missed. A mother had been trying to keep a lid on a toddler with the old Cheerios bribe, which meant there were babies in the house that weekend. That also meant the old neighborhood hadn't given up.

I smiled, and I believe that the old man we were burying got a smile out of that too.

There wasn't much need to check the pamphlet rack as I left. After all, I had discovered once again the truth of what my mother had told me so many years ago: The Church will always be there.

.

.

.

.

.

.

CHAPTER SEVEN

{Charity}

Charity—love—is the third of the theological virtues, and it is the most important part of the life of a believer. Love is the core of all Christian teaching, because God is love. He commands that we love him and love each other, and he gives us the grace of this virtue that we might accomplish both in our lives.

Christian love is the source of our freedom from the pains and sorrows of this life. With love and in love, we can bear all that is bitter in the pilgrimage. Every Christian activity should be a result of love and have no other point but to end in love.

My friend's brother was dying, victim of the same genetic disease that had killed his father years before. Mark had been essentially confined to bed for over a year, and the hospice people had a difficult time explaining why he was still alive.

I had come from Pennsylvania to visit at the beginning of the holiday season and was greeted like a pilgrim who had been gone far too long. The mother had been through her own story lately:

a ticker that was nearly down for the count with cancer to add fuel to the fire. But she was insistent on living long enough to bury her son and to see her other son through the empty times that she so clearly remembered from her husband's death.

She took me in to see Mark, and he seemed to recognize me, though it was hard to tell any longer. The television was on to keep him company. He liked old science fiction shows, the cooking wars on the Food Channel and college football. I didn't know what to say to him, so I said something ridiculous about how well he looked. I think he knew that he had looked better.

Mother and I went to the kitchen, where my old friend was putting together a chicken salad lunch. He did most of the heavy lifting for everyone, and I was worried that he was getting very tired. Taking care of his dying brother didn't allow for many breaks.

Only a moment after we slipped into congenial talk about movies, the Church and the world, Mother slipped out to check in the bedroom. Her dying son had started having seizures that morning, and they were keeping an ever-closer eye on him. She came back to tell us that they had begun again, making her arms rigid and rolling her eyes back in vivid pantomime.

The hospice nurse was called, and I got up to leave. "Nonsense," my friend said. "We like to talk. It helps." So I stayed and talked, while they quietly rotated in and out of the kitchen to monitor their dying son and brother. The word *consolation* comes from the Latin *consolatio*. It means "being with the other in their solitude." So that it ceases to be solitude.

The arriving nurse was taken to the bedroom, where symptoms were discussed and medicines strategized. She came to the kitchen and explained the situation with the usual shrug. "It could be today; it could be months. I've given up trying to figure him out," she said with a smile. "He's one tough customer." His mother actually beamed at the compliment.

Feeling that I was getting in the way, I tried to make my departure, but I was again blocked. "Hang around," the nurse said. "You do them good."

So I hung around. The doorbell rang again, and a kid was selling a new phone service. It reminded me of the Jimmy Breslin story in which his buddy died and the television kept playing. Life goes on.

The seizures eased as the afternoon waned. They thanked me for staying as long as I did, and I thanked them for allowing me to be there, because I had caught a glimpse of divine love that day.

Chuckles and Charity

We think of charity as giving out a little spare change. But in the classic theological sense, charity is love and very specifically divine love—meaning that it is a gift of God. Charity is a reflection in our lives of God's love, a love we can't earn or purchase. It is our vocation to live that love as best we can and to mirror it all the moments of our lives.

The guy behind the counter used to sell me Chuckles and talk for a minute about yesterday's ball game. Chuckles are those jellied candies that are one reason among many that I occupy more space than I did in my salad days. The guy took pride in the fact that he always had my Chuckles, and if I picked one of the last packages, he'd always say, "Don't worry. I've got them on order. We'll have a full boat tomorrow." And he always did.

After a while habits—and tastes—change. I stopped dropping by. It had probably been a year or more when I got hit with a

Chuckles rush, and since I was in the neighborhood, the little shop beckoned. The counter, however, was now manned by a kid engrossed in a magazine of questionable morality. He didn't look up when I asked him if the other fellow still worked there. "Dunno," he offered, and that was that. And they didn't have any Chuckles.

So many people pop in and out of our lives. Everyone from the best friend not seen since high school to the waitress who served a hot cup of coffee with a smile this morning and made the day a little better. They can be as fleeting as the guy behind the steering wheel who waves open a spot in rush hour traffic, as casual as the guy selling stamps at the post office or as permanent as the aunt who died thirty years ago but always had a good word for a kid who wasn't her own.

The faith is incarnational, lived in the company of humanity. We are all connected by grace, and we never know this side of heaven the lives we may have touched and all the lives that have touched us. And how many more opportunities we will have.

A flight attendant on a short-hop flight on a jet no bigger than a minute said a few words of assurance to me after I nervously outlined in a couple of sentences my plans for changing my career that day. Years later I still remember her kindness, though I'm sure she hasn't a clue.

Somewhere a statistician must have calculated how many people we meet in ways large and small in our lives. It must be tens of thousands, if not many, many more. And every moment has a chance for grace.

A woman of a certain age—her grandchildren are grown—calls me now and then to talk about everything and nothing in partic- ular. But it had been a few years when the phone rang and she announced herself, starting the conversation as if we had spoken fifteen minutes before. Among other things she told me that she had given up smoking. "I also lift weights," she said.

"Lift weights?" I asked, stunned.

"Yeah, you should see my guns." She cracks me up.

Lucy Van Pelt of the *Peanuts* comic strip once explained that it is our task in life to make people happy. She was not happy: "Someone's not doing their job!"

I try to keep that in mind as the day goes by. None of us know when we get up in the morning exactly what the day will bring. But one thing can be certain: Each day is a point of grace, and grace will be encountered in the people with whom we will share that day.

Jean Paul Sartre, the depressing French existentialist, argued that hell was other people. But as the years go by, I realize that hell must be an eternity alone, cut off from God and his greatest creation.

When we talk about charity—divine love—we are not describing some sappy sentimentalism from an oldie-but-goody on the radio, an eighth-grade crush or our lusting after an object of our obsession. Charity is that glimpse of the divine love that exists through our Creator in our lives and in our world. People are God's tender mercy in our lives, our chance to live out—and experience—his charity. Even if they just remember to order the Chuckles.

Lucy was closer than she thought to defining charity.

A Little Scripture

A moment of honesty here—reading the classic books we are supposed to read can be a deadly chore. Try as I might, I found

Dickens's *Oliver Twist* a crashing bore. Melville's *Moby Dick* was great fun until I encountered roughly two hundred pages of nineteenth-century scientism on the various breeds of whales and their habits.

Our friend Dante, even when describing in lurid detail the pains of hell, can tell us more about thirteenth- and fourteenth-century Florentine politics and his arguments with the secular business of the popes than we would ever want to know. And when he finally encounters the ever-chaste love of his life, Beatrice, to take us through the rest of his story, a lot of us begin to nod off. Dante's descent through hell gives us a thrill; his ascent through heaven can be a bit of a snooze.

But as Dante neared the end of his pilgrimage, John asked him to define charity, or divine love. Dante answered:

> The being of the world and my own being,
> the death He died so that my soul might live,
> the hope of all the faithful, and mine too,
>
> joined with the living truth mentioned before,
> from that deep sea of false love rescued me
> and set me on the right shore of true Love.
>
> I love each leaf with which enleaved is all
> the garden of the Eternal Gardener
> in measure of the light he sheds on each.[1]

Which is Dante's way of saying that "God is love, and he who abides in love abides in God, and God in him" (1 John 4:16).

The First Letter of Saint Paul to the Christian community at Corinth is a treat for anyone interested in what life was like for the early Christians. The Christian community at Corinth, scholars tell us, was founded by Saint Paul himself in AD 51—less than twenty years after the crucifixion and resurrection of Jesus.

Corinth was only a hundred years old but was a thriving trade center in southern Greece, larger by far than ancient Athens. It had been rebuilt on the site of the old Corinth, wiped out two centuries earlier by an angry Roman consul who killed every man in the city and sold the women and children into slavery. So it goes.

But Corinth had been repopulated over the last century, filled with people from every corner of the Roman Empire. It was also filled with every kind of pagan cult and every kind of sin.

Paul had been successful in Corinth among the poor laboring classes. But while on a mission, he heard reports that the community was breaking into factions, following different leaders in different directions. The community was spending more time fighting with each other than spreading the Good News of Jesus Christ. It was a mess.

So Paul wrote to them, addressing both the minutiae of their individual issues and their jealousies. After describing how each person has a role in the community according to his or her gifts, he defined what he called "a still more excellent way" to live faithful to their baptism. It is a quote from Paul read—and promptly forgotten—at almost every wedding ceremony I've attended:

> If I speak in the tongues of men and of angels, but have not love, I am a noisy gong or a clanging cymbal. And if I have prophetic powers, and understand all mysteries and all knowledge, and if I have all faith, so as to remove

mountains, but have not love, I am nothing. If I give away all I have, and if I deliver my body to be burned, but have not love, I gain nothing.

Love is patient and kind; love is not jealous or boastful; it is not arrogant or rude. Love does not insist on its own way; it is not irritable or resentful; it does not rejoice at wrong, but rejoices in the right. Love bears all things, believes all things, hopes all things, endures all things.

Love never ends. . . .For now we see in a mirror dimly, but then face to face. Now I know in part; then I shall understand fully, even as I have been fully understood. So faith, hope, love abide, these three; but the greatest of these is love. (1 Corinthians 13:1–8, 12–13)

In the Company of Men

I had been asked to give a talk, and I was taking a quick breather outside the church hall before things got under way. The talk was for a Holy Name Society celebration in Beaver County, Pennsylvania, and the parking lot was already packed.

A car pulled up while I was getting my thoughts in order, and a lady rolled down the driver's side window. "Is this where they are having bingo?" she asked. "Nope," I answered, and worried about a world where a crowded church parking lot could only mean one thing.

My talk went OK. In my allotted fifteen minutes I managed to bring in the Holy Father, Thérèse of Lisieux, Cardinal John Newman, the Old Man and the guy who delivered milk door-to-door when I was a kid. That's a good batting order.

Then the awards program began. The fellow next to me whispered that the key to getting a good crowd was to give out a lot of awards, because the whole family of each recipient would have to come. Even the kids and grandkids came back into town to see the Old Man get his recognition.

It was fun. The guys would get their picture taken with their award, then pull some notes from their jacket pocket to make sure they thanked everybody who had to be thanked. One fellow had his two typewritten pages, a torn-off note from a newspaper, the program of the event and a napkin with some last-minute scribbling. The stuff kept falling off the dais. But then when he finally started, he forgot about all that and just spoke from the heart about family, faith and service to the Church.

The guys weren't getting awards for what someone might call the big stuff. No one was recognized for saving any lives or running into burning buildings. What most of these guys accomplished were the small things done in love. They helped bake bread for parish celebrations, pitched in to keep the church building in order, taught CCD classes, started prayer groups. They were guys the pastor could count on when something had to get done. They were all about the love that "bears all things, believes all things, hopes all things, endures all things."

Thérèse of Lisieux explained love pretty well. She lived in a small corner of France in a convent, doing the simple chores—cooking, cleaning, washing. She would die at the age of twenty-three. About as unremarkable a life as you can imagine. Understanding that most of our lives are but little moments for gentle service, she wrote in *The Story of a Soul* about getting into the habit of holiness. There are no moments too small to be sanctified, she told us.

Most good people don't live the faith on any grand stage. They live the faith in their neighborhoods, teach the faith to their young, evangelize those they touch in their small corner of the world.

As I watched the parade of guys yanking nervously at their ties and struggling through their embarrassed thanks in front of an audience who knew everything about them anyway, I realized how blessed I was to be in the company of men. It beat bingo any day of the week.

A Sacrament

The old *Catechism* taught us that a sacrament is "an outward sign instituted by Christ to give grace." Sacraments are our encounters with divine love that give us the grace to live lives of charity. If you keep your eyes open, you can catch the truth of that.

Hoosiers anticipate a springtime of bone-chilling drizzle, broken only when the meteorological forces drag in a colliding warm front to spawn a few tornadoes. But on this late April day, the temperatures reached into the high sixties, and the sky was as blue as it ever gets over northern Indiana.

We were there to celebrate a wedding. I had been to any number of weddings before, but this one seemed special. The sacramental nature of it all was so real that I could feel it in my bones.

The sacraments are commonly misunderstood as rituals for celebrating, acknowledging or mourning specific passages in our lives. Instituted by Christ, the sacraments are so much more. They are real and actual sources of grace in our lives. They are avenues of an intimate connectedness to God.

The Church believes that our lives can be great. While most of society opts for the lowest common denominator and is pretty well convinced—and convinces us—that it is the best anybody can do, the Church keeps telling us that we can do better. The Church believes in humanity and believes that we can be saints.

That is the odd contradiction between the way the Church is portrayed by society and the way the Church is. The chattering classes paint the Church as the great naysayer. The Church, they say, harbors an unrealistic portrait of humanity, denying to its adherents the accepted normalcy of life in these trying times. It is this culture of mediocrity that invents rationalization, the ability to excuse the inexcusable. It is a culture that has simply redefined deviancy, arguing that only the most loathsome of sins is worth worrying about. It's a culture that asks to be led into temptation and expects little delivery from it. It's a culture that tells us that sanctity and goodness are ideals to admire in principle rather than realistic goals to achieve. It's a culture that has lost a sense of love.

Recovering alcoholics in the early stages take great pride in doing things that sober people do regularly: get to work on time, clean the house, walk the dog, pay the bills. They have failed at these simple human chores for so long that doing them and doing them right is an achievement. While we grant them the right to gloat over these early victories, we know that the path to continued sobriety has to get beyond that. They have achieved only the first level of regaining their souls and must keep growing.

When it comes to the way we live, the culture has reduced us to that same first step and tells us that we never need grow beyond that. The basic excuse is that the ordinary is good enough. Yet the Church just doesn't buy it. The Church knows that we can be good and great. It doesn't say that it is easy, but it says it can be done.

The Church also tells us that we don't have to do it alone. In fact, it tells us that we can't do it alone. The Church believes that through the life of the sacraments, we are connected to God in such a way that greatness in this life is right here, right at our fingertips. We don't have to settle for the ordinary, for the good enough. With God, through the grace of the sacraments, anything is possible.

On that picture-perfect Hoosier Saturday, I witnessed a young couple exchanging their vows in the sacrament of matrimony. This was no simple ritual, no public acknowledgement of a contract, no marking of the passage of time. This was so evidently a moment of sacrament, an infusion of grace that would make a difference in these two souls. It was enough to make a grown man weep. Which I did, of course, when I was pretty certain no one would notice. That's what you do when you are the father of the bride.

Running Late

"You're a day late and a dollar short," I remember the nun telling me in sixth grade when the book report was finally turned in on a book I had never read. This defined my academic career before and after. You would think as an adult that I would do better. Generally speaking I do not.

My wife had been staying with my daughter and her husband in Detroit, through what would turn out to be the last week of her pregnancy. I stayed behind in good old Chippewa Township, Pennsylvania, schlepping off to work in the morning and hanging around the house at night—lots of television reruns that week.

When the call came that the action had commenced, I threw a bag together and started on the five-hour drive like a bat out of hell, though my particular bat of a beaten-up Toyota coasts along safely no matter what my intentions might be. About twenty-five minutes north of Toledo, Ohio, I got the call on the cell phone that I was a first-time grandfather twice over: Twin boys had just graced us. Extraordinarily blessed to be the father of twins, I was now the grandfather of twins as well. An oldies station was playing "Lean on Me" when I heard the news.

My wife said that when the contractions really got going, my daughter was all smiles and gave her the thumbs up. That's the way my kids are. My son calls from Army boot camp to tell me what a great time he is having; my daughter gives the high-sign and a big grin when she's a first-timer about to deliver twins.

So I'm a day late and a dollar short, just as the good sister warned me. Actually I would only be about forty-five minutes late. Yet my grandkids have arrived, and I'm fighting Detroit traffic in a car desperately in need of a wash and an oil change. But I'm a happy and thankful guy.

When my wife was expecting twins, I spent the whole pregnancy worrying about whether I could stomach changing a diaper. Within twenty-four hours of getting them home, I could change a dirty diaper while eating pepperoni pizza.

In the back of my mind during my daughter's pregnancy, I feared I would be one of those maudlin guys who'd get all lumpy about old age once she made me a grandfather. Not a chance. Too much of a miracle to get all sloppy and introspective.

In Michael Perry's *Population: 485*, he writes about his service as a volunteer fireman and EMT in a small Wisconsin town. He describes setting up a beer tent on a Sunday morning for a fund-raiser at a softball tournament. The games start early, and soon a guy saunters over for a cold one. It's not even 9 AM, and the beer tent is not set up for business, but Perry digs out a cup and pours the fellow a beer. Just as the guy is about to take a chug, somebody smacks a long fly ball and, startled, he snaps his head around to watch the outfielder make the catch. He takes his sip, then opines, "Little early in the mornin' for softball!"[2]

Everything is context.

I look at my grandkids and remember my grandfather—their great-great-grandfather. He was born well before the Wright brothers flew, and his granddad well before the Civil War. The mystery of time, and the unseen connections from generation to generation, hit you square between the eyes when you see your grandchild for the first time.

Perry writes about the birth of his small town volunteer fire department, when the town bought "one double 35 gallon Chemical Engine" in 1905. Then he comes across an old photo of one of his co-volunteers taken years before, when he first started. It was at a party for a fifty-year veteran, and that old vet would have used that first chemical pumper. Perry is struck by the "quirky narrative that weaves itself through generations. The events arrange themselves along a communal timeline. The community is the constant.... The old-timers hand down equipment and stories, show up occasionally when we're short-handed, but most of all they help us recognize that time—*our time*—is transient."[3]

We used to talk more about the "communion of saints." It is the intimate union between the Church Militant (we the living), the Church Suffering (the poor souls in purgatory) and the Church Triumphant (those in heaven). We got away from that language—informally if never officially. In fact, "triumphalism" became kind of a postmodern pejorative, implying a cocksure

Catholic attitude about truth that was not a part of contemporary thinking.

As I look at my grandkids, I feel the blessed pull of the ages, that intimate connection not just to me but to my father and his father and his father's father. They are all connected through the ages of a family's history, some of which is long forgotten but still living in them. And that's the mystery of the Church. But all the more deeply, all the more universal in Christ, all the more real in divine love.

I do confess that in the last forty-five minutes of that drive to Detroit, a lot of loved ones dropped by for a visit. My grand-parents, even the grandfather who died a few months before I was born, as well as the grandfather who lived with us for seven years when I was a kid and told long stories that made me laugh; my father and mother; aunts and uncles, cousins and in-laws. All gone but all there with me as a beat-up car covered the last few miles.

God is great, and life is good when we get to see that spark of his divine love. Even when we are a day late and a dollar short.

One More Road Trip

"So faith, hope, love abide, these three; but the greatest of these is love" (1 Corinthians 13:13).

When my friend's brother died, I was out of town. I couldn't get back in time for the funeral, so I failed to bury the dead. I got on the road later to visit the family and pay my respects.

Mark's last days had not been easy for the family. Though death can be kind, dying can be brutal. He had been incapable of swallowing in the final weeks, and his veins were too weak for intravenous feeding. His brother would place water in a syringe and drip it onto his tongue. "I was thirsty and you gave me drink" (Matthew 25:35). Then Mark slipped away one night.

I was greeted again like the wandering soul. My friend and his mother looked tired, so I offered to treat for dinner. My friend and I went to a classic little Hoosier restaurant where the sautéed mushrooms are out of this world and you can hear the cook giving the servers what-for as you wait for your peppercorn steak with the angel-hair pasta on the side. Don't be turned off by the gas pumps that are right next to the place. I've generally found that in Indiana that's a good sign.

In the old days this was the place I would take friends who were coming in on business trips. The whole staff knew me, and when we came in, though I hadn't darkened the door in a handful of years, I was acknowledged as if I had been there last Tuesday. The waitress—the same waitress who was there the very first time I gave them the business—brought me a diet drink without even asking, then slapped open her pad and asked, "Whatcha havin' tonight, boys?" We told her what we were having, then ordered a meal to go for my friend's mother.

Back at his house the conversation was as it always was: old stories, new stories; old friends, new friends. They described Mark's funeral and all the lives that he had touched. They spoke of hospice nurses going back to Mass after a long absence, of people moved to tears who had never known Mark personally but had prayed for him as part of an almost universal network that had grown up around the family. They had people praying next door and in New York, California and Rome.

"That's why he died peacefully," his mother said. "I was amazed by the outpouring of love and prayer for a fellow that most of these people never even met."

They asked me if I wanted to see him. His ashes were in an urn in his old bedroom, waiting for the time that he could be buried back in Hawaii next to his father. I touched the urn, wished him God's peace and choked up a bit. I'm doing that more lately. We all get by on divine love, though we don't often get the chance to see it so perfectly expressed in one life and one death.

"May He support us all the day long, till the shades lengthen and the evening comes, and the busy world is hushed, and the fever of life is over, and our work is done. Then in His mercy may He give us a safe lodging, and a holy rest and peace at the last."[4]

And in the End

It was Tuesday evening now, the sun long set. Another day, another dollar.

The gas station in my little town sits at about the highest elevation. That means that when I open the door to get out to pump some gas, the wind hits me like a closed fist. Lord, it does get cold in Pennsylvania.

Dante found himself in a dark wood when he wandered off the path of righteousness at the beginning of the *Divine Comedy*. Here I am at a gas station filling up an old Toyota so I can get on the road again in the morning. The pilgrimage continues.

Dante's pilgrimage was through hell, purgatory and heaven. Ours is through a different kind of dark wood. Dante looked to the heavens and saw the stars of the virtues—prudence, fortitude, temperance and justice; faith, hope and charity. They are stars never seen on earth, he wrote. But we can feel them around us.

I look up at the stars as the gas pump counts my dollars. It might be cold, but it is a beautiful February night. The insight is really very simple:

At this point power failed high fantasy
but, like a wheel in perfect balance turning,
I felt my will and my desire impelled

by the Love that moves the sun and the other stars.[5]

NOTES

Introduction: The Virtues

1. Dante Alighieri, *Inferno*, Canto I, 1–3, 10–12, in Mark Musa, ed., *Dante Alighieri's Divine Comedy*, volume one (Bloomington, Ind.: Indiana University Press, 1997), p. 3.
2. Quoted by Pope Benedict XVI, Address to an Interacademic Conference on "The Changing Identity of the Individual," January 28, 2008, available at: www.vatican.va.
3. Stephen King, *Bag of Bones* (New York: Simon and Schuster, 1998), p. 45.
4. William Shakespeare, *As You Like It*, Act II, Scene VII, in *The Portable Shakespeare* (New York: Penguin, 1983), p. 502.
5. Pope Benedict XVI, Address to the Participants in the International Symposium of Secular Institutes, February 3, 2007, available at: www.vatican.va.

Part One: The Cardinal Virtues
Chapter One: Prudence

1. Quoted in Alice Hogge, *God's Secret Agents: Queen Elizabeth's Forbidden Priests and the Hatching of the Gunpowder Plot* (New York: HarperCollins, 2005), p. 64.
2. Quoted in Hogge, p. 80.
3. Quoted in Hogge, p. 84.
4. *Inferno*, Canto III, 35–36, in Musa, volume one, p. 25.
5. *Inferno*, Canto XVII, 10–12, in Musa, volume one, p. 157.
6. James Salter, "The Writing Teacher," *The New York Times*, book review, May 8, 2005, available at: www.nytimes.com.
7. From *Adoro Te Devote*, ascribed to Thomas Aquinas, Gerard Manley Hopkins, trans., available at: www.seadoration.org.

Chapter Two: Fortitude

1. Leigh Montville, *The Big Bam: The Life and Times of Babe Ruth* (New York: Doubleday, 2006), p. 364.
2. Montville, p. 29.
3. Quoted in Paul Dickson, *Baseball's Greatest Quotations: An Illustrated Treasury of Baseball Quotations and Historical Lore* (New York: HarperCollins, 2008), p. 475.
4. *Inferno*, Canto XXIV, 46–51, in Musa, volume one, p. 229.
5. *Inferno*, Canto XXIV, 60, in Musa, volume one, p. 229.

6. Quoted in Maryknoll International, Biography of Bishop James E. Walsh, July 29, 2000, available at: www.KC4076.org.

7. "Prayer of Saint Francis of Assisi," in James D. Watkins, ed., *Manual of Prayers* (Rome: Pontifical North American College, 1998), p. 323.

8. John Newman, "The Mission of My Life," *Manual of Prayers*, pp. 232–233.

Chapter Three: Temperance

1. *Purgatorio, Canto* XI, 100–106, in Musa, *Dante Alighieri's Divine Comedy,* volume three (Bloomington, Ind.: Indiana University Press, 2000), p. 109.

Chapter Four: Justice

1. *Inferno, Canto* III, 103–105, in Musa, volume one, p. 29.

2. Quoted in Antonia Fraser, *Faith and Treason: The Story of the Gunpowder Plot* (New York: Doubleday, 1996), p. 266.

3. *Paradiso, Canto* X, 3–6, in Musa, *Dante Alighieri's Divine Comedy,* volume five (Bloomington, Ind.: Indiana University Press, 2005), p. 93.

4. *Paradiso, Canto* XIV, 25–27, in Musa, volume five, p. 133.

Part Two: The Theological Virtues
Chapter Five: Faith

1. George Weigel, *Witness to Hope: The Biography of Pope John Paul II* (New York: Harper Collins, 1999), p. 262.

2. Quoted in Weigel, p. 262.

3. Pope John Paul II, *Redemptor Hominis*, Encyclical Letter "The Redeemer of Man," March 4, 1979, no. 1, available at: www.vatican.va.

4. Weigel, pp. 289–290.

5. *Paradiso, Canto* V, 74–78, in Musa, volume five, p. 47.

6. *Paradiso, Canto* XXIV, 64–65, 70–73, in Musa, volume five, p. 237.

7. Quoted in Rheta Grimsley Johnson, *Good Grief: The Story of Charles M. Schulz* (Kansas City: Andrews and McMeel, 1989), p. 137.

Chapter Six: Hope

1. Prayer of Saint Teresa of Avila, *Manual of Prayers*, p. 251.

2. Myles Connolly, *Mr. Blue* (Albany, N.Y.: Richelieu Court, 1990), p. 72.

3. *Paradiso, Canto* XXV, 66–69, 73–75, in Musa, volume five, p. 247.

4. Pope Benedict XVI, *Spe Salvi*, Encyclical Letter on Christian Hope, November 30, 2007, no. 2, available at: www.vatican.va.

Chapter 7: Charity

1. *Paradiso*, *Canto* XXVI, 58–66, in Musa, volume five, pp. 255, 257.
2. Michael Perry, *Population: 485: Meeting Your Neighbors One Siren at a Time* (New York: Harper Perennial, 2007), p 26.
3. Perry, p. 35.
4. Cardinal John Newman, "A Daily Prayer," *Manual of Prayers*, p. 230.
5. *Paradiso*, *Canto* XXXIII, 142–145, in Musa, volume five, p. 331.

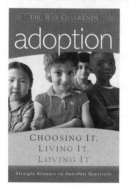
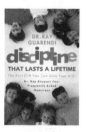

CHRISTOPHER WEST

Good News About Sex & Marriage:
Answers to Your Honest Questions About
Catholic Teaching
Christopher West
Foreword by Charles J. Chaput, O.F.M., CAP.,
Archbishop of Denver

Christopher West is a research fellow and faculty member of the Theology of the Body Institute. Good News About Sex & Marriage presents Catholic Church teaching about human sexuality and marriage in a fresh, appealing and convincing manner.

Order# T16619 • ISBN 978-0-86716-619-4 • $12.99

EDWARD SRI

Men, Women and the Mystery of Love:
Practical Insights from John Paul II's Love
and Responsibility
Edward Sri

Father Karol Wojtyla (Pope John Paul II) published Love and Responsibility in 1960, the fruit of his pastoral work, particularly among young people. His analysis of the true meaning of human love is life-transforming and practical, shedding light on real issues between men and women. Edward Sri unpacks the contents of this great work, making it accessible to every reader.

Study questions with each chapter make this a valuable resource not only for individual personal reading but also for small group study.

Order# T16840 • ISBN 978-0-86716-840-2 • $12.99

FATHER PETER JOHN CAMERON, O.P.

Jesus, Present Before Me
Meditations for Eucharistic Adoration
Father Peter John Cameron, O.P.

Through meditations, prayers and probing questions for reflection, Father Peter John Cameron, O.P., invites you to see beyond appearances and enter into the mystery and miracle of Jesus present in the Eucharist. "You were made for this presence," Father Cameron says.

Jesus, Present Before Me includes thirty separate eucharistic meditations, eucharistic reflections on the twenty mysteries of the rosary, a eucharistic colloquy, a litany and a Way of the Eucharist, all designed to help you offer your time of adoration wholeheartedly, without weariness or distraction.

Leatherette cover • Order# T16857 • ISBN 978-0-86716-857-0
$18.99

MIKE PACER

Prayers for Catholic Men
Mike Pacer

A pocket-sized guide for daily prayer and victorious living, this book includes both original and traditional prayers to help you focus on God throughout the day and in times of special need. Prayers that get to the point, combined with brief encouraging reflections, provide a framework in which you can open your heart and mind to the will of God. Whatever your situation—from praying for the grace to cope with an annoying person to praying for the strength to overcome despair—Prayers for Catholic Men will help you stay the course, confident that no matter what life throws at you, God is in charge.

Leatherette cover • Order# T16881 • ISBN 978-0-86716-881-5
$12.99